U-BOATS

9-5-88

To Daddy,
Happy 53rd Birthday
Love, Karl

ALSO BY EDWIN P. HOYT

U-Boats Offshore

Guadalcanal

Airborne:
The History of American Parachute Forces

The Glory of the Solomons

The Kamikazes

Submarines at War:
The History of the American Silent Service

Blue Skies and Blood:
The Battle of the Coral Sea

Closing the Circle:
War in the Pacific

The Battle of Leyte Gulf

The Invasion Before Normandy:
The Secret Battle of Slapton Sands

The Militarists:
The Rise of Japanese Militarism Since World War II

Japan's War

McGRAW-HILL BOOK COMPANY   NEW YORK   ST. LOUIS

U-BOATS

a pictorial history
by Edwin P. Hoyt

SAN FRANCISCO   TORONTO   HAMBURG   MEXICO

N.B.: Lest the rank designations given various officers in this book be confusing, note:

1. The officers who survived through the war were constantly being promoted. Thus an officer might be lieutenant in one chapter and lieutenant commander in another.

2. The German system of naval ranks differs from the American. The word commander *(kommandant)* in German was used to signify a U-boat captain no matter his rank. In English we have the same system: the captain of a submarine may be a commander or a lieutenant commander. I have used the words captain and skipper to signify that position, as well as referring to the officers by their naval rank as translated into English.

All photographs reproduced in this book are from
the Stiftung Traditionsarchiv Unterseeboote, Westerland, Sylt, except those of U.S. naval ships
and airplanes. Those photos are courtesy U.S. Navy.

1 2 3 4 5 6 7 8 9 DOC DOC 8 7 6

ISBN 0-07-030620-6

LIBRARY OF CONGRESS CATALOGING-IN-PUBLICATION DATA

Hoyt, Edwin Palmer.
   U-boats : a pictorial history.
   1. Submarine boats—Germany.   2. Germany.
Kriegsmarine—Sea life.   3. World War, 1939–1945—
Naval operations, German.   I. Title.
V859.G3H68   1987   359.3′257′0943   86-10382
ISBN 0-07-030620-6

BOOK DESIGN BY LINEY LI

Contents

The monument at Möltenort. This column, near Kiel, was erected by the survivors of the U-boat wars in memory of the 28,000 U-boat sailors killed in action in World War II. In all the U-boats suffered 85 percent casualties, and of the 1,150 U-boats commissioned, over 900 were sunk before war's end.

Introduction

This book provides a close look at life in the German U-boat forces in World War II. It dramatizes the history of the U-boats, their designers, officers and crews with stories of life at sea and ashore, of their exploits on patrol and under attack, of successful raids and sunken missions, many of which will be unknown to most readers of military history. In so doing, *U-boats* provides insights into the German prosecution of this war at sea and gives an unusual look inside an enemy world.

The vast majority of photographs in this book come from the Stiftung Traditionsarchiv Unterseeboote now housed at the Naval Air School in Westerland, the rental paid by the German Submariners Association. Eleven volunteers help the founder maintain this archive, which takes its name from the U-Boat Memorial located at Möltenort near Kiel, on the North German Baltic Coast. The archive contains 17,000 photographs, plus virtually everything written about U-boats in German, English, French, and other languages. The archive contains details about the operations and history of most of the 1,174 U-boats commissioned by Germany during the Second World War. For the most part the photographs were placed in the archive by survivors of the U-boat command or by the families of men who went down with their ships.

The director of the Stiftung Traditionsarchiv Unterseeboote had asked to see the text and captions of this book. When he received proofs he became furious over the chapter on Nazis in the German submarine service and demanded that his name be removed from the book. This was done, but he continued to object, saying that no sea officer and no other naval officer had ever been associated with the NSDAP, this being, he averred, forbidden by naval tradition. He also criticized the author's use of the British Naval Interrogations' reports of prisoners and other material about Nazis in the German service as sources in the book. The author continues to believe that British Naval Intelligence knew whereof it spoke. It has been a long time since Hitler's empire collapsed, and every year the number of old Nazis is decreased by attrition and by forgetfulness. That is probably just as well, considering the changes in the world, but let us not forget how things were in 1935–45.

U-BOATS

1. Between the Wars

Until the end of the nineteenth century, the "torpedo boat" was regarded as the most deadly of small naval craft. Under certain conditions, torpedo boats could threaten even the mighty battleship fleets which every navy considered to be the first line of its defenses. Torpedo boats accomplished the great Japanese naval victory at Port Arthur, which opened the Russo-Japanese War. In 1900 six navies owned a total of 10 submarines with another dozen under construction. By 1914, the number of submarines afloat had grown to 400. When war broke out, the Germans very quickly saw that they could not match the British on the sea, fleet for fleet, and they adopted a policy of attrition. The submarine soon came to play a major role. In the German navy most of the naval resources of the war from 1914 to 1918 were devoted to the submarine. The German word for submarine is *Unterseeboot* (undersea boat), and it was quickly shortened in military slang to *U-boot,* whence we get the English "U-boat."

At the beginning of World War I, in 1914, the submarine was regarded as a military weapon. Only when the Germans had lost most of their surface raiders did they turn seriously to the submarine as a raider of commerce. This change brought some immediate difficulties. The surface raiders could easily chase a merchant ship, overhaul it, take the crew aboard the raider, sink the merchantman, and ultimately deliver the merchant-ship crew either to a neutral vessel or put them aboard a seaworthy vessel to sail to safety. That was the practice and it was the rule of sea warfare. But when the submarine came along, the rules no longer fit the game. The submarine was much smaller than its quarry, and subject to ramming and sinking. There was scarcely room for the crew aboard the vessel, particularly on the German submarines, which were constructed with an eagle eye to utilization of space. So the crews of the merchant ships could not be accommodated.

The result was the revolution of sea warfare, which ended in unrestricted submarine campaigns. The horror of sinkings without notice, of the abandonment of crew and passengers of merchant ships to the dangers of the sea, began with the sinking of the steamer *Lusitania* in 1915. This policy shocked the world and was abandoned by Germany for a time. But as the war went on, the German admirals saw that their only hope of victory was to stem the tide of supply coming to Great Britain and France from the rest of the world, and the unrestricted submarine warfare campaign was begun again and lasted for the final twenty-one months of the war.

Between the two world wars, idealists again had their say in the matter of submarine warfare. The British wanted to abandon the submarine altogether and outlaw it as a weapon of war. The Americans and the Japanese opposed and quelled that effort. The result of this debate was a lame international policy, embodied in the London Protocol of 1934, which set down a group of rules for submarine warfare:

1. The submarine must surface before attacking.

2. Crews and passengers had to be guaranteed safety. They could not be abandoned in small boats on the high sea. Either they had to be taken aboard the submarine (which was impossible in terms of space), or the submarine captain had to hail a neutral ship to take them aboard (most improbable), or the ship had to be let go.

3. Merchant ships were not to be armed.

4. Merchant ships were not to use their radios to call for help or warn other ships at sea about the submarine.

As these rules were laid down, the most practical of naval authorities knew they were bunk, and that they would never survive the early days of any war. Chief among the skeptics were Winston Churchill, a member of the British House of Commons, and Commander Karl Dönitz of the German navy, a submarine specialist who had been one of the most successful U-boat captains in World War I.

Dönitz came from a family of military men and evangelical pastors. Perhaps the characteristics of these callings are not so far apart, for Dönitz possessed the qualities of both: a fine regard for Prussian discipline and a constant preoccupation with every aspect of submarine construction and operations—a concern that was like a religion to him.

Before World War I, Dönitz served aboard SMS *Breslau*. During the war, he progressed to submarine skipper and squadron commander. The end of the war left Germany without submarines, and theoretically without the further technical skill to build them. But the German engineers went to Holland. In 1922 they established the firm Ingenieurskaantor voor Scheepsbouw at the Hague. This firm was funded by German money from industrial firms in the Ruhr. Dr. Hans Techel was the technical head of the firm, and Commander Hans Blum was "sales manager." They secured orders from several countries in South America, Spain, Finland, and Turkey. In 1930 they took the first disassembled U-boat to the Port of Åbo in Finland, a boat built to designs developed by the German U-boat force in World War I, and there German officers and technicians assembled it and taught the Finns how to use it. At Amsterdam they built a pair of 500-ton boats for the Turks. These submarines were delivered to Turkey by German officers, seamen, and engineers. Thus was the German skill in U-boat building and operations preserved.

By 1931 they were building big boats. The 1,965-ton boat *E-1* was built that year and sent to Spain.

Dönitz was one of the handful of officers retained in the shattered German navy of the postwar period. His career apparently moved away from involvement with the outlawed U-boats to follow traditional lines. He became captain of the cruiser *Emden*. But always in Dönitz's mind was the shadow of the U-boat.

To rebuild their submarine forces, the Germans had to move very subtly in these days after the Treaty of Versailles had theoretically stripped them forever of the power to make war.

On January 30, 1933, President Hindenburg handed Adolf Hitler his appointment as Chancellor of the German Republic. Five months later, on June 25, 1933, at Kiel, the tiny German navy established the Antisubmarine Warfare School, as innocent a beginning for a new U-boat force as anyone could imagine. Wasn't it natural for even Germany to be allowed such defensive training? Britain and France had submarines;

Germany had none. Who could object? A dozen officers and about sixty petty officers and enlisted men established this school, for training in navigation and the other aspects of naval art and science. Thus was the U-boat force constituted. It was all done very quietly. The officers and men trained in civilian clothes, and in small groups. No attention was paid them by the media or the high command. Practical work with U-boats was carried out by sending the men up to Åbo in Finland during the summer months.

On the grounds of the Deutscher Werke and the Germania Shipyard in Kiel, several small hangars were erected. They were surrounded by fences and heavily guarded, and no one without authority was allowed inside.

What went on inside them was protected by the navy with extremely tight security precautions. They were building submarines, quite illegally under the Versailles Treaty: *U-1* to *U-6,* 250-ton boats of the Finnish prototype. These were built for use in coastal waters. They displaced 254 tons, they were equipped with two diesel engines for propulsion on the surface and two electric motors for underwater movement. They could make 13 knots on the surface and 7 knots underwater. The armament consisted of three torpedo tubes, and one twenty-millimeter gun. They carried crews of twenty-five men. As they were completed, the expanding school at Kiel provided the manpower. Germany's naval rebuilding program began here with the redevelopment of the U-boat.

In 1936, the need for total secrecy ended with Hitler's march into the Rhineland, bluffing the French and the British, who could have stopped him then had they shown the moral fiber upon which Winston Churchill was urging they draw. Hitler had already swallowed Austria. After the Rhineland occupation, the French and British were so thoroughly outbluffed that it was not hard to persuade them to the next step: the legalization of German rearmament. One result was the Anglo-German naval agreement which set potential German naval might at 35 percent of the British. Here, then, was an official international agreement that gave Germany the basis for building ships. Three days later the Germans established a program to build 24,000 tons of U-boats.

The agreement was signed on June 16, 1935. Then, immediately, the secret hangars were opened. *U-1,* the first U-boat of the modern class, was brought out, ready to launch. She was fitted out, along with those that came swiftly after her, and on July 28, 1935, *U-1* began her first patrol, just forty-two days after the signing of the new naval treaty. Obviously it paid to be forearmed. Thereafter every fourteen days another U-boat joined the German fleet, until the first flotilla of six Type II-A U-boats was completed.

All this while Karl Dönitz was deep in the councils of the naval authorities who were planning the reconstruction of the U-boat arm. The summer of 1935 found Commander Dönitz, captain of the cruiser *Emden,* setting out on a cruise into the Indian Ocean. Commander Dönitz had been involved in the new U-boat program on several levels. Aboard the *Emden* was Lieutenant Godt, who would be Dönitz's right-hand man in the development of the new U-boat corps.

Even as they sailed on their cruise, the Germans at home were at work building a better boat—Type II-B. The new 500-ton class of trans-atlantic U-boats was also under construction.

On the long cruise, far from the inquisitive eyes of the British, Commander Dönitz worked out many of his strategic and tactical ideas. Dönitz's plans for the U-boat arm went far beyond those of any other submarine specialist in the world. From his own experiences as a U-boat captain in World War I, Dönitz was certain that the convoy system would be Britain's answer to attack at sea. He had to produce a counter to the convoy, and he could expect that the British would have done as much to perfect the devices for surface detection and combat against U-boats as the German specialists had done during the peacetime years to improve the U-boats' security, speed, radio methodology, and weapons. The cruise to the East ended, Dönitz brought the cruiser back to Wilhelmshaven, and there he was met by Admiral Raeder, commander of the German navy, who told Dönitz that his next duty was to be chief of U-boats. He would be responsible for the building and operation of the German U-boat fleet. The fleet was not much at the moment; with the commissioning of *U-7, U-8,* and *U-9* that September, Dönitz had a flotilla of nine boats. It was designated the Weddigen Flotilla, in honor of the best U-boat commander of World War I, Otto Weddigen.

By the end of 1935, Dönitz had perfected his theory of "wolf pack" attacks on convoys. In 1937 the technique was "proven," as far as the Germans were concerned, in war games in the Baltic Sea.

Most of the early U-boats of the 1930s were those small coastal craft of about 250 tons. Theoretically they were to be used for "defense" of the North Sea and Baltic coasts of Germany. Actually they were to scour the North Sea and the Baltic and lay mines around Britain when the time came. Dönitz hoped the time would not come until the 1940s, when he expected to have 300 U-boats at sea, including the 500-ton craft and even larger boats. With these, and the U-boat force he intended to build, he said, he could assure Germany of a victory over the British, no matter how quickly they implemented their convoy system.

This thin-lipped Prussian naval officer, totally dedicated to duty himself, set down a standard for his U-bootwaffe that was easily the highest in the German navy. From the beginning Dönitz expected to be called upon to provide more and more captains for a growing force of submarines, and so every man accepted into the service in these early days was put down as potentially a captain, and the rigorous training all underwent was designed to make them strong leaders and commanders. Dönitz was promoted to Kapitän zur See in recognition of his service so far.

The officer candidates were first sent to a training school on the island of Dänholm near Stralsund. There they began the most rigorous sort of training. They were up at 6:00 A.M. winter and summer. In winter the temperature sometimes fell to 40 degrees below zero. Only the toughest survived the rigorous course of exercise and study that was imposed on them. The idea was to test character first of all, and inevitably some men fell by the wayside. There were even suicides among the candidate corps, and many a gloomy day was spent by every candidate, thinking he was failing. But once this immense hurdle was passed, the candidates emerged with new vigor and a greatly increased self-confidence. To Kiel they went next, to serve aboard the three great sailing ships, *Gorch Fock, Albert Schlageter,* and *Horst Wessel.* In cold and heat they stood watches on the bridge, climbed the rigging in the storms, and learned the hard ways of sail. Once this second rigorous course was ended, the young men were officially called sea cadets and their uniform jackets bore a star and one thin band of gold braid.

All the U-boat crews, from captain to the lowest apprentice seaman, were volunteers. In the 1930s, as Dönitz built his force, it was known that the most exclusive military service in Germany was the U-bootwaffe. The volunteers could expect the hardest training, the most severe discipline.

In the first six months the volunteers were given a general course in seamanship, with many examinations, both physical and mental, to weed out the unfit. Then they went to the boat where their real training began. They were taught to shoot and to use the weapons of the U-boat. Every boat had to make sixty-six forays to practice diving, torpedo operations, and the use of the deck gun. They learned to dive by daylight and by night, emergency dives, very deep dives. And in all this the crews were timed. The idea was to produce a crew that could move a boat in any manner almost automatically with the greatest of speed and competence. On this their lives would depend in wartime.

Especially hard and long was the training of the watch officers and the men who would stand watches with them, for on these men depended the fate of the boat when she was on the surface. Four hours was a long time to stand bridge watch, to remain alert for that first sign of an aircraft or that first wisp of smoke that indicated a ship, or that telltale stick in the water that might be an enemy submarine on the prowl.

The U-boat service was very much "the silent service." Civilians were not allowed aboard the U-boats or even near them except on official business. Neither, at first, were the Nazis who had begun to politicize the army and navy. Dönitz brushed them off with the argument that every effort must be devoted to combat efficiency; there was no time for any political consideration. He managed to convince the politicians that this was in the best interests of the Third Reich. Aboard the U-boats, there were plenty of pictures of girls, but scarcely any of Adolf Hitler. Thus, in the beginning, the German submarine leader was able to develop a force of supremely competent technicians and fighters, whose loyalty was to the German homeland and to Dönitz's leadership.

The year 1935 was spent working on the *Rudeltaktik* (the wolf-pack strategy). Nine more boats were added to the flotilla that year. In war games in the summer of 1937 in the North Sea, Dönitz did convince Raeder and the other high officers of the German fleet that the wolf-pack tactic was sound.

But the growth of the U-boat fleet was too slow for Dönitz to establish the wolf pack as the basic submarine technique of the moment. He had to fall back on the old system of sending individual boats on individual patrols. There were not enough boats, and the boats were too small. In the summer of 1936, the Germans began building the Type VII, the Atlantic U-boat, of 600 tons with four bow torpedo tubes and one tube aft.

Dönitz set up his headquarters in the old German naval base of Wilhelmshaven, which was ideal for his purposes since it was located on the North Sea, much closer to England than Kiel, which was on the Baltic. The inner harbor at Wilhelmshaven was turned over to the U-boats, for fitting out and diving. The U-boat force then began to train with intense fervor, directed from the Dönitz headquarters on Tote Weg (Dead Alley), which runs between the Wiesen and Äckern districts of Wilhelmshaven, not far from the old port, which was turned into a submarine basin.

Dönitz equipped the new headquarters with the most modern in communications equipment before he moved his operations there from Swinemünde in the Baltic. All of Captain Dönitz's world was set up on a system of charts which divided the seven seas (and the rest) into small numbered and lettered grids. Almost at a glance, Dönitz could send a U-boat into a position to patrol a particular fifty square miles. In terms of the area of the earth, this was indeed a very strict measure of control. From Tote Weg he would control all his boats, and that was understood by all his captains. There was none of this business of sending a submarine captain off on patrol without knowing precisely where he was going and precisely what he was doing. And as 1939 began, Dönitz was getting ready. With him was Godt, now Dönitz's chief of staff, and a Fregattenkapitän, and Lieutenant Öhrn, who was one of the best and brightest in the service. There, also, was Lieutenant von Stockhausen, a genius of communications, who had established the system by which Dönitz would control his U-boats throughout the world. This meant high-speed radio transmitters and receivers, the most advanced among the world's navies, and total radio discipline by the boats at sea. From the outset, radio would play an enormous role in the U-boat war and the Germans would have the initial advantage because of their advanced communication system.

As the training and the building continued, Dönitz was already looking forward to a large, more powerful boat that could easily cross the Atlantic, remain on station for several weeks, and return. This was the Type IX U-boat, which would displace 750 tons, and be capable of traveling 12,000 miles.

What Dönitz wanted was his fleet of 300 U-boats, which would enable him to maintain 100 boats at sea all the time, he estimated. And with that force, he could control the North Atlantic and the approaches to England.

At the end of May 1938, Hitler began making plans for a great war, based on the designation of England as the coming enemy. Dönitz kept promoting his plans, but higher naval authority believed in a different concept, and Hitler was persuaded to spend a good deal of the Reich's resources on the building of a surface fleet of powerful cruisers and "pocket battleships." German naval strategy since the 1800s had been based on the concept of raiding enemy commerce on the surface, and the idea had not died in the 1914–18 war, for, in truth, several of the raiders had been very successful and the surface-fleet men could make a case for the naval defeat based on insufficient armament and insufficient fuel capacity for the raiders. In this atmosphere, given an Adolf Hitler to whom the whole naval effort seemed small potatoes, Dönitz did not make much headway with his 300–U-boat concept. He tried again in 1938, but was again rebuffed. The Z Plan of the German navy for construction called for the production of 237 U-boats by 1948, which would give Dönitz his 300 boats. That was a far cry from what Dönitz wanted, but as a loyal German naval officer he had to live with what was granted him. So, when the crisis came in the summer of 1939, Dönitz found himself with 56 U-boats in service. Of these, only 22 were available for immediate service in the Atlantic.

1-1 The old navy. They looked like admirals but they were only commanders. Commander Karl Dönitz, left, with Commander Otto Hersing of the tiny German navy that existed between the wars. The lieutenant commander in the middle is not identified. **1-2** Launching the *U-36*. One of the first of the Type VII U-boats, launched on December 16, 1936, with her entire crew. The civilian in the center is unidentified. **1-3** Commander Karl Dönitz in 1935. He was then captain of the German cruiser *Emden,* on a long voyage that took the ship into the Indian Ocean. On their return, Dönitz was appointed commander of U-boats and told to prepare for the coming war.

1-1

1-2

1-3

1-4

1-4 Laying the keel for one of Dönitz's U-boats. Until 1936, the U-boats were built in secret sheds, but then, when the Allies agreed to the rebuilding of the German navy, it was brought into the open. **1-5** The German U-boat flotilla at Kiel, 1938. **1-6** *U-39* leaving harbor for trials. This Type VII boat represented Dönitz's early dreams. It was faster on top of the water than many of Britain's escort vessels (see text). Underwater it could send its deadly torpedoes from three tubes. On the surface its deck gun could fight anything smaller than a destroyer. The device on the top of the bow is a net-cutter. **1-7** Winter at Wilhelmshaven. These are some of the little 250-ton "canoes" that were the first modern U-boats of the World War II navy. **1-8** Shooting the sun. The best way to learn was to do, so the quartermasters were taught aboard the U-boats to use the sextant.

1-5

1-6

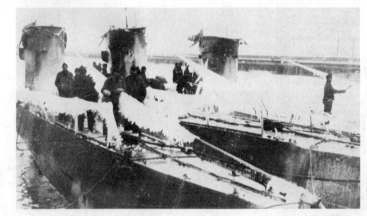

1-7

1-8

1-9

1-10

1-9 Barracks at Flensburg. This was the home of the U-boat cadets as they trained in the most arduous fashion for their future within the U-bootwaffe. **1-10** The Seamen's Church, Wilhelmshaven. This church honors all of Germany's naval dead, but the U-boat men have a special feeling for it, since Wilhelmshaven, more than any other place, was the home of the German U-boat fleet. **1-11** Coming up from the deep, using the escape vest. **1-12** Part of the training of a U-boat man was to go down into the deep, don an escape vest, and come up through the water as he would have to do if he was to survive the sinking of his U-boat. Later the U-boat corps used a submarine that had been sunk in shallow water for such training.

1-11

1-12

1·13

1·14

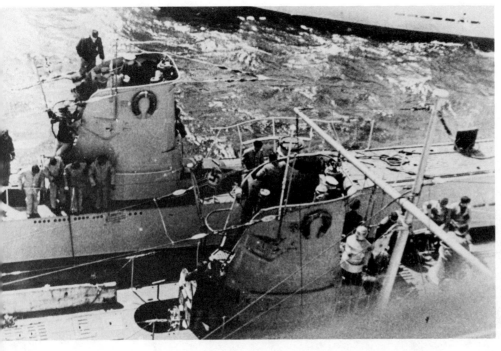

1-13 Tactical training of U-boat officers in the school program. They are using Dönitz's world grid system (note characters D50E between the commander's arms). Using that system, Dönitz could spot any one of his U-boats (and victims) anywhere in the world. **1-14** One of the main U-boat training centers was located at Pillau. The cadets in summer uniform march under the direction of a petty officer. **1-15** The little Type I and Type II U-boats were used for training of U-boat men at Pillau. These are officer candidates learning the boat. **1-16** The *U-9* under construction at Kiel. She was one of the first ten boats built by Dönitz under the World War II building program, a Type II-B.

1-17

1-18

1-19

1-20

1-17 The *U-9* at sea. The picture was taken before the outbreak of hostilities. After war began, all insignia were painted out, replaced by individual boat symbols that gave away no military secrets. **1-18** The conning tower of *U-9* with starboard running light and radio antenna. The Maltese cross is the traditional German military symbol. The eagle with swastika was added by the Nazis. **1-19** *U-30* in the North Sea on maneuvers, 1938. Note the beerdrinker on the left. **1-20** Skipper Julius Lemp on the bridge of the *U-30,* a Type VII boat. **1-21** Lieutenant Lemp and friends. Lemp is second from left. The man on the right is not from the U-boat service.

1-21

1-22

1-22 The *U-30*'s deck gun in winter.
1-23 The U-boat flotilla at Kiel,
before the war. **1-24** The crew of
the *U-43* at Bremen in the summer
of 1939. In the front are the
U-boat's officers. This was an
"official" photo, made for the crew
to send home to their families, and
the numbers identify the enlisted
men.

2. War!

September 1939: Hitler ordered the attack on Poland; Britain responded to live up to her alliance with Poland. The war began. At 1:30 on the afternoon of September 3, 1939, Chief of Staff Godt handed Lieutenant von Stockhausen the message written by Dönitz: "Begin hostilities against England immediately."

Everyone had known it was coming. In August Dönitz had staged what was in effect an alert, although it might have been more. His U-boats had virtually surrounded England, proving it could be done. Now, they had gone out again, and this time it was not a game. Two hours before unleashing his U-boats, Dönitz had reminded all his captains of their rights and responsibilities under the Hague Convention and naval treaty of 1934. Troop transports and merchant ships were subject to seizure as prizes. Enemy warships could be sunk without warning. Passenger ships carrying passengers were not to be disturbed unless they were engaged in military activity, and how was any U-boat commander to know that from the end of a periscope? And yet just such a matter became the most important of all on that first effective day of the sea war.

One of the bright young men of Dönitz's command was Lieutenant Fritz-Julius Lemp. His record had brought him the command of *U-30*, one of the Type VII-A Atlantic boats, the best that Dönitz had. Lemp had been assigned to one of the most important sea-lanes, off the Irish coast, and he had reached his assigned grid area and was on patrol when the messages from Dönitz came. He saw a ship that afternoon. She was a large ship, and as Lemp saw her, memories rushed through his mind. During all the months at school, Dönitz's young officers had been cautioned against English traps. One of the most deadly of the traps (in

Dönitz's mind, although not in reality) was a Q-ship, a merchant ship that had been made into a warship by the addition of heavy guns and depth charges. During World War I, Q-ships had accounted for the loss of several U-boats, but those were in the early days, before the U-boat captains had learned to shoot first and ask questions later. Q-ships had fallen out of fashion, and although there was talk about reviving them in World War II, nothing much happened, because the war was moving too quickly and the British had much more on their minds.

The second hidden enemy was the armed merchant cruiser, which was usually a passenger ship turned into a warship. Such ships had been used with considerable success by the British in the last war, particularly against armed German surface raiders. And they would play their role in this second war, too. So the captains were warned against these "auxiliary cruisers" as well. Dönitz's standing orders to his captains included several prohibitions regarding treatment of merchant ships: no crewman was to go on board any steamer that was held up; gunfire was to be used to halt ships, make them steer the proper course, make them stop trying to use their radio. Dönitz also warned his captains against believing what they saw: "On every occasion using gunfire it must be borne in mind that nearly all enemy ships are armed and that neutral markings afford no proof of the actual neutral nationality of a steamer. Remain therefore a good distance away."*

And this day, although Dönitz's messages had warned against attacking passenger vessels, Captain Lemp saw this ship as something more than just a passenger vessel, and without warning he sank her.

What a dreadful beginning for the U-boat force! With all the talk about laws of war that had been floating around Europe for five years, they were right back to where they had been in 1915 when a U-boat had sunk the *Lusitania*. Or would have been, had not the German Propaganda Ministry in Berlin pulled out all the stops. To be sure, when the word came through the airwaves that the ship Lemp had sunk was the liner *Athenia*, Captain Lemp did not report to Dönitz as he was supposed to do. He played possum and hoped desperately that the whole nightmare he had stepped into would go away. So Berlin, questioning Wilhelmshaven, was able to say that Dönitz knew nothing about the sinking of a liner by a U-boat (although Dönitz knew in his heart what

*Standing War Order No. 153.

had happened and through that incomparable grid system must have known immediately precisely who it was who had done the deed). But without an admission, Berlin was able to clothe itself authoritatively in the voice of rectitude and claim that the British had done the dirty job as a stroke of psychological warfare against Germany. This claim echoed around the world. Several factors combined to give the German claim some credence and to make it hard for the straightforward British denials to have effect. First, the American ambassador to Britain, Joseph Kennedy, was no friend of the British, and his personal investigation of the event (undertaken because Americans died aboard the *Athenia*) left much to be desired. Then, too, some German-Americans and some "limey-haters" were aboard, and they made a number of wild claims, including one that the first mate of the *Athenia* said she was carrying war materials. Consequently, in all the charges and countercharges, the truth of the sinking of the *Athenia* was concealed for months. The U.S. Department of State was nearly a year in concluding that the Germans had, indeed, done the job.*

For a whole year the Germans had kept the water muddy. The Germans played their propaganda so forcefully that many neutrals (including Americans) really believed that the *Athenia* had been destroyed by Britain.

Hitler's first reaction was fury, because one of his earliest warnings to the navy had been at all costs to do nothing that would tend to bring the Americans into the war. He demanded the head of the offending U-boat captain. He told the navy that they were to sink no more passenger vessels under any conditions.

Dönitz's reaction was not the same as Hitler's although it had even more far-reaching consequences. Dönitz had never believed in the naval treaty of 1934, which had set up all those impossible rules for U-boat warfare. But Dönitz also recognized the need for Germany to show a

---

*Not until September 2, 1940, one day short of the first anniversary of the sinking of the *Athenia*, did a State Department official announce "the strong presumption" that a German torpedo had sunk the liner, rather than the "British destroyers" that the Germans accused in their year-long propaganda campaign. How times have changed! In the spring of 1986, when a terrorist bomb killed four American passengers aboard a TWA jet liner, the U.S. government was not in the least bashful at casting the responsibility in the direction of Colonel Qaddafi of Libya. But in 1939, it must be remembered, the American people were not nearly so used to violence on the international scene, and, as in 1914, there was still much pro-German and anti-British feeling in the United States.

clean bill in the navy war. So he put out orders of his own to the effect that the rules were to be obeyed as strictly and as cheerfully as possible. Thus, after the initial brutality of the submarine attack on the liner, the German conduct of the war at sea became very gentlemanly in those autumn months of 1939, and remained so. Many a British ship was sunk afterward, but, if the sea made it possible, the Germans would surface, talk to the men in the lifeboats, give them provisions and liquor, and directions to the nearest land. A good many British seamen came home from a sinking with a high regard for their enemies, which is precisely what Dönitz wanted. It was also excellent fodder for the German propaganda machine.

Meanwhile, unavoidably, Winston Churchill, the First Lord of the British Admiralty, set up the conditions that would lead to the ultimate abandonment of this "gentlemanly warfare" by the U-boat force. By 1939 every vessel of any size was equipped with radio, and when the war broke out the ships were advised to take every anti–U-boat precaution. If attacked, they were to send a special signal *SSS SSS SSS* instead of the old *SOS SOS SOS.* This new signal *SSS* meant attack by submarine, and its sound on the air alerted every British warship and aircraft that could hear, and caused rapid movements in the shore commands that could dispatch assistance. Thus the British were technically violating the old naval agreement about submarine warfare.

When Churchill learned of the sinking of the *Athenia,* the news confirmed his gut feeling that the Germans could never be trusted and he vowed to arm every passenger and merchant ship on the seas. His insistence became final two days later when Lieutenant Herbert Schultze sank the British steamer *Royal Sceptre.*

Schultze reported that the British ship had broken the rules of submarine warfare. His *U-48* had overhauled the ship, which was flying no flag, and had ordered it to stop. But instead of stopping, the *Royal Sceptre* had speeded up, run up the Union Jack, and begun sending that *SSS SSS SSS* signal, which would draw to the scene any and every warship around. So Schultze had sunk her without ado, and never a look back. In fact, Schultze was among the most gentlemanly of the German captains. After the sinking of the *Royal Sceptre,* which had women and children aboard, it was not long before *U-48*'s skipper spotted the steamer *Browning* in the area. He surfaced, saw that the *Browning* had picked up the women and children from the lifeboats of the *Royal Sceptre*, and let her go.

But the action against the *Royal Sceptre* had triggered Churchill's reaction. The Admiralty began immediately to arm merchant ships. As these armed ships took to the water, and engaged the submarines when they attacked, as many did, the "unfair" British use of weapons was immediately reported to Dönitz, and he put it down in his records as another reason to abandon the charade of restricted submarine warfare when the time came.

To bolster the war spirit of the German people, Dr. Goebbels's propaganda ministry needed heroes and the U-boat men were in the forefront. Lieutenant Günther Prien sank a number of ships, and was lionized at home. Lieutenant Otto Schuhart's *U-29* sank the British carrier *Courageous*, an accomplishment that also became a propaganda victory for Dr. Goebbels. It also taught the British the folly of using a fleet aircraft carrier on antisubmarine patrol, which they were doing at the time.

Unnoticed by the propagandists was another group of U-boat commanders, working in the North Sea in the little 250-ton Type I and Type II U-boats, laying mines around the British ports. In fact, the mines did more damage in the early months of the war than the highly publicized ship sinkings. But that fact was barely known to Captain Dönitz's headquarters, so well did the British keep their secrets. And the men who undertook this dangerous and thankless duty were unknown outside the U-boat force itself.

Just about then, the British had their first little victory over the U-boats, when Lieutenant Glattes's *U-39* attacked the carrier *Ark Royal*. Glattes did not sink the carrier, but the British destroyers accompanying her did sink the U-boat, and the crew went into captivity. A few days later the British also sank Lieutenant Franz's *U-27* and saved most of the crew to go into prison camp.

But the U-boats were taking their toll. In the first month of war they sank fifty-two ships. Lieutenant Lemp came home about the end of that first month and had to admit that he had sunk the *Athenia*. Fortunately for him Hitler had cooled down by then, and Goebbels's propaganda ploy had so thoroughly confused world opinion that it would have been worse to admit than to forget. So Lemp was slapped on the wrist (given one afternoon in close arrest to contemplate his sin) and the records of *U-30,* by Dönitz's orders, were carefully expunged of all evidence of the act. The propaganda campaign accusing the British continued unabated. It was many months before it became common knowledge that Lemp had sunk the *Athenia,* although of course the U-boat corps knew from the beginning.

That fall of 1939, Dönitz dearly wanted to try out his wolf-pack tactics, but he did not have the ship power to do it. He had the organization: Commander Hartmann in the *U-37* was designated Chief, Atlantic Group. But the dream would have to wait.

In October 1939 came an event that strengthened Dönitz's position immeasurably within the naval establishment and with the German public.

It began on Sunday, October 1, aboard the *Wechsel,* the headquarters ship of the U-boat command in Wilhelmshaven harbor. Commander Sobe, Lieutenant Wellner, and Lieutenant Prien were sitting in the lounge, discussing tactics and adventures. Wellner remarked that on his recent patrol in the Orkneys he had come by Scapa Flow, and found the entrance wide open. Scapa Flow was the major British naval base for its home fleet, just in the process of being shored up, and Lieutenant Wellner had discovered a British secret: that the blockships ordered for all the channels into Scapa Flow anchorage had not yet been put in place.

The matter was brought to Dönitz's attention, and he examined his charts, saw what Wellner meant, and put the matter up to Lieutenant Prien, who was ready to go out on patrol. Did Prien think he could get inside Scapa Flow, torpedo the British at anchor, and get out again? Prien was given the charts and took them off with him for an afternoon of study. He returned to Dönitz to say yes, he thought he could do it. Thus was the order given for the invasion of Britain's most important fleet anchorage. Prien's *U-47* sailed on October 8, and four days later reached the Orkneys. Prien took her down to the bottom, and lay there the rest of the day. He called the crew together and told them that this very night they were going to move into Scapa Flow. After dark, he brought the *U-47* to the surface and carefully conned her through these shallow, difficult waters, virtually under the eyes of the British home fleet.

Inside, Lieutenant von Varendorff, the second watch officer, spotted a battleship lying at anchor. It was HMS *Royal Oak*. He also saw a second ship behind the battleship, which he identified as the battle cruiser HMS *Repulse*. The identification was wrong: the second ship was the carrier *Pegasus*.

Working in, Lieutenant Prien fired three torpedoes at the ships. He hit the *Royal Oak* squarely, but the *Repulse* was unhurt. What matter! In a few minutes the *Royal Oak* turned over and sank, taking down one admiral, twenty-three officers and 800 men.

Swiftly, in the darkness, Lieutenant Prien made his way out of the tortuous passage and in the confusion got clean away. As soon as possible he reported to Dönitz. The German propaganda machine had another victory to exploit. Grudgingly it was conceded by the British that the *Royal Oak* had been sunk in what should have been Britain's best-protected waters. The resulting investigation wrecked several British naval careers, and caused the movement of the British home fleet around to the Atlantic side of England.

Here is the log of the *U-47* for the voyage from Kiel to Scapa Flow and back:

10/8/39

11:00. Heligoland Bight.
Wind southeast 1.* Cloudy.

Left port [Kiel] on special operations. Operational Order North Sea No. 16, through Kiel canal, Heligoland Bight, and Channel 1.
Exact positions cannot be given as under special orders all secret documents were destroyed before carrying out of order.

10/9/39

South of Dogger Bank.
Wind, south-southeast 4–5.
Overcast. Very dark night.

Lying submerged. After dark, surface and proceed on our way. Met rather a lot of fishing vessels.

*Force 1 = 7 knots, Force 2 = 14 knots, etc.

10/10/39

North of Dogger Bank.
Wind, east-southeast 7. Overcast.

During day lay submerged. At night continued on course.

10/11/39

Devil's Hole.
Wind east-southeast 7–8. Overcast.

As on previous day.

10/12/39

Wind southeast 7–6. Overcast.

During day lay submerged off Orkneys. Surfaced in the evening and came into the coast in order to fix exact position of ship. From 10:00 P.M. to 10:30 the English are kind enough to switch on all the coastal lights so I can obtain a most exact fix. The ship's position is correct to within 1.8 nautical miles, despite the fact that since leaving Channel 1 there was no possibility of obtaining an accurate fix, so that I had to steer by dead reckoning and soundings.*

10/13/39

East of Orkney Islands.
Wind, north-northeast 3–4.

Light clouds, very clear night, northern lights on entire horizon. It is a very eerie night. On land everything is dark, high in the sky are the flickering northern lights, so that the bay,

---

*Quite properly, Dönitz's captains of 1939 were proud of their navigation, the result of the strenuous German naval training program. They were probably the best navigators of any naval force in the world.

surrounded by high mountains, is directly lit up from above. The blockships lie in the sound, ghostly as the wings of a theater.

At 4:37 A.M. lying submerged in 270 feet of water. Rest period for crew. At 4:00 P.M. general stand-to. After breakfast at 5:00 P.M., preparations for attack on Scapa Flow. Two torpedoes are placed in rapid loading position before tubes 1 and 2. Explosives brought out in case of necessity of scuttling. Crew's morale splendid. Surfaced at 7:15 P.M. After warm supper for entire crew, set course for Holm Sound. Everything goes according to plan until 11:07 P.M. when it is necessary to submerge on sighting a merchant ship just before Rose Ness. I cannot make out the ship in either of the periscopes, in spite of the very clear night and the bright lights. At 11:31, surfaced again and entered Holm Sound. Following tide. On nearer approach, the sunken blockship in Skerry Sound is clearly visible, so that at first I believe myself to be already in Kirk Sound, and prepare for work. But the navigator, by means of dead reckoning, states that the preparations are premature, while I at the same time realize the mistake, for there is only one sunken ship in the straits. By altering course hard to starboard, the imminent danger is averted. A few minutes later, Kirk Sound is clearly visible.

I am now repaid for having learnt the chart beforehand, for the penetration proceeds with unbelievable speed. In the meantime I had decided to pass the blockships on the northern side. On a course of 270° I pass the two-masted schooner which is lying on a bearing of 315° in front of the real boom, with 45 feet to spare. In the next minute the boat is turned by the current to starboard. At the same time I recognize the cable of the northern blockship at an angle of 45° ahead. Port engine stopped, starboard engine slow ahead, and rudder hard to port, the boat slowly touches bottom. The stern still touches the cable, the boat becomes free, it is pulled around to port, and brought onto course again with difficult rapid maneuvering . . . BUT . . . we are in Scapa Flow.

10/14/39

12:27 (midnight). It is disgustingly light. The whole bay is lit up. To the south of Cava there is nothing. I go further in. To port, I recognize the Hoxa Sound coast guard, to which in the next few minutes the boat must present itself as a target. In that event, all would be lost.

12:55 (midnight). At present south of Cava no ships are to be seen, although visibility is extremely good. Hence decisions: south of Cava there is no shipping; so before staking everything on success, all possible precautions must be taken. Therefore, turn to port is made. We proceed north by the coast. Two battleships are lying there at anchor and further inshore, destroyers. Cruisers not visible, therefore attack on the big fellows. Distance apart, 3,000 yards. Estimated depth, 22 feet.

12:58 (midnight). Impact firing. One torpedo fixed on the northern ship, two on southern. After a good 3.5 minutes, a torpedo detonates on the northern ship; of the other two nothing is to be seen.

1:21 A.M. About! Torpedo fired from stern. In the bow two tubes are loaded. *Three torpedoes from the bow.* After three tense minutes comes the detonation on the nearer ship. There is a loud explosion, roar, and rumbling. Then come columns of water, followed by columns of fire, and splinters fly through the air. The harbor springs to life. Destroyers are lit up, signaling starts on every side, and on land 200 yards away from the shore cars roar along the roads. A battleship has been sunk, a second damaged, and the other three torpedoes have gone to blazes. All the tubes are empty. I decide to withdraw because

1. with my periscope I cannot conduct night attacks while submerged. (See experience on entering.)

2. on a bright night I cannot maneuver unobserved in a calm sea.

3. I must assume that I was observed by the driver of a car which stopped opposite us, turned around, and drove off toward Scapa at high speed.

4. nor can I go further north, for there, well hidden from my sight, lie the destroyers which were previously dimly distinguishable.

1:28 A.M. At high speed both engines we withdraw. Everything is simple until we reach Skilaenoy Point. Then we have more trouble. It is now low tide, the current is against us. Engines to slow and dead slow, I attempt to get away. I must leave by the north through the narrows because of the depth of the water. Things are again difficult. Course 058° slow—10 knots. I make no progress. At high speed I pass the southern blockship with nothing to spare. The helmsman does magnificently. High speed, ahead both, finally three-quarters speed and full ahead all out. Free of the blockships—ahead a mole! Hard over and again about, and at 2:15 we are once more outside. A pity that only one was destroyed. The torpedo misses I explain as due to faults of course, speed, and drift. In tube 4, a misfire. The crew behaved spendidly throughout the operation. On the morning of 10/13, the lubricating oil was found to have 7 to 8 percent of water in it. All hands worked feverishly to change the oil, i.e., to get rid of the water and to isolate the leaking point. The torpedo crews loaded their torpedoes with remarkable speed. The boat was in such good form that I was able to switch on to charge in the habor and pump up air. Set southeast course for base.

2:15 A.M. I still have five torpedoes for possible attacks on merchantmen.

6:30 A.M. 57° 58' north, 01° 03' west. Lay submerged. The glow from Scapa is still visible for a long time. Apparently they are still dropping depth charges.

7:35 P.M. East-northeast 3–4. Light clouds, occasional rain, visibility bad toward land, otherwise good.
     Off again, course 180°. This course was chosen in the hope that we might perhaps catch a ship inshore, and to avoid *U-20*.

10/15/39

6:00 A.M. 56° 20′ north, 0° 40′ west.

Submerged and lay at 210 feet. From 10:00 A.M. onward, depth charges were dropped from time to time in the distance. Thirty-two depth charges were definitely counted. So I lie low, submerged, until dusk.

6:23 P.M. Wind northeast, sea 4, swell from east, cloudy, visibility good.

Surfaced. On surfacing, Norwegian steamer *Meteor* lies ahead. Radio traffic from the steamer is reported in error from the radio office. I therefore fire a salvo far ahead of the steamer, which is already stopped. The steamer is destined for Newcastle on Tyne with 238 passengers. Steamer immediately allowed to proceed. It is reported later by the radio officer that the steamer did not make any signals.

10/16/39

54° 57′ north, 2° 58′ east. Wind north-northwest 2–3, visibility good.

General course 180°. Submerged in the Dogger Bank. Three drifting mines sighted, 54° 58′ north, 2° 56′ east. No measures taken owing to the proximity of fishing vessels. Proceeded submerged throughout the day.

6:56 P.M. 54° 51′ north, 3° 21′ east. Wind northwest 2, light clouds, visibility good.

Surfaced. Course 128°. Steered course of 128° into Channel 1.

10/17/39

4:04 A.M. Channel 1 passed. From 4:04 to 4:47 chased Fishing Vessel Escort Ship No. 808, gave recognition signal eight times, no reply received. This fool did not react until Very signals were used at a distance of 500–600 yards. With such guardships, an incident such as my operation could occur in our waters also.

11:00 A.M. Entered port Wilhelmshaven III.

11:44 A.M. Tied up.

3:30 P.M. Crew flown to Kiel and Berlin.

10/20/39

4 P.M. Crew returned.

6:30 P.M. Sailed for Kiel.

11:30 P.M. Met an armed fishing trawler at anchor with riding lights in the stretch between Elbe I and Elbe II. I pass him with darkened ship at a distance of 40 yards. Apparently he sees nothing, because no call for recognition signal is made.

10/21/39

1:20 A.M. Tied up at Brunsbuttel lock.

1 P.M. Tied up at Holtenauer lock.
    Operation completed.

On October 17 Prien's *U-47* entered Wilhelmshaven harbor to be greeted by Captain Dönitz and Admiral Raeder, commander of the fleet. There, on board the *U-47*, Admiral Raeder announced the promotion of Captain Dönitz to Rear Admiral. The officers and men of the *U-47* were given leave, and wherever they went they were lauded by their countrymen. Lieutenant Prien was taken up to Berlin by Admiral Dönitz, and they were given an audience by Adolf Hitler, who pinned a medal on the brave captain. Dönitz took this occasion to bring up his U-boat building program. How Hitler hated being forced by circumstances to make quick decisions! But Dönitz had the tide of public opinion with him just then, and Hitler darkly conceded that there must be an increase in the number of U-boats built. Gratefully, Admiral Dönitz slid away from his unpredictable chief and returned to Wilhelmshaven to redouble his efforts.

Maneuvers did not always result in victories for the U-boat force. Some boats were attacked and sunk by enemy destroyers and patrol craft. Harder to bear in a way was when the boats were lost the other way: when a U-boat set out on patrol and at some point dropped out of communication, and was never heard from again. But in these early days of the war there was not much of that. This was the halcyon period, when victory for the U-boats seemed very likely on both sides of the English Channel. The sinkings were many, and the losses of U-boats few. On the sea as well as on the land, Hitler seemed omnipotent. The British did have a defense program, centered around their Asdic electronic homing device. The Asdic emanated a sound which bounced back to the receiver aboard the patrol craft as a ping, and the frequency of the pings and their loudness indicated to the trained operators where Asdic was encountering metal. Of course some of these Asdic contacts were wrecks, but a satisfying number of them were submarines, and as the war progressed British skill with the Asdic device made life more difficult for the U-boats.

In the beginning of the war, the British knew that the convoy system developed in World War I must be the answer to the U-boats. But the task of forming real convoys was not that simple; the British were very short of convoy patrol craft. They needed to use destroyers for this work, but did not have enough of them. Very soon, Winston Churchill began a program of building small craft, called corvettes, suitable for antisubmarine work. But in the fall of 1939 these vessels were just being laid down, and so the Germans were virtually uncontested, having a real field day, *"ein grosser Paukenschlag"* they called it—a great drumbeat.

The British convoys were more effective on paper than at sea. In the North Sea, they were so short of warships that none at all were used, except on military convoys. Theoretically, the merchantmen in the North Sea were protected by aircraft, but there were not enough airplanes either, and they could not be used to fly over the convoys, but maintained patrol areas. The system gave the little 250-ton U-boats every advantage.

On the other side of England, where the deep water of the Atlantic lay, and the hunting was for big ships, the British had their troubles too. It was here that Dönitz hoped to make use of his wolf-pack tactics, even though he did not have enough boats available to sustain this sort of warfare.

On October 7, several U-boats of the Second U-Boat Flotilla set out on patrol: Lieutenant Hartmann's *U-37,* Lieutenant Dau's *U-42,* Lieutenant Schultze's *U-48,* Lieutenant Sohler's *U-46,* Lieutenant Gelhaar's *U-45,* and Lieutenant von Schmidt's *U-40.*

Lieutenant von Schmidt's boat hit a mine in the English Channel and sank with all hands. But the other boats went out, under the overall command of Hartmann. At first they encountered individual ships, sailing alone. Schultze's *U-48* sank the French tanker *Emile Miguet.* That same day Captain Hartmann sank the Swedish steamer *Vistula,* which he said was carrying war goods for the British, and the Greek steamer *Ares.* Then Schultze and Dau found British outbound Convoy No. 17d and sank three ships. On October 14, Lieutenant Gelhaar found Convoy KJF 3, and in rapid succession torpedoed three ships. That same day Schultze sank another.

Guided by information intercepted from the British, on October 16 Dönitz ordered the group of U-boats to move south. On the move to the new operation zone, on the morning of October 17, Sohler's *U-46* encountered Convoy HG 3, bound for Gibraltar. Sohler gave the co-ordinates, and so *U-37* and *U-48* were able to come up. That was what the wolf pack was all about; one submarine to find the convoy, and track it, and bring the others in. Sohler torpedoed the 10,000-ton steamer *Yorkshire,* but she did not sink. But the next day up came *U-37* and *U-48* and Hartmann sank her. An hour later Sohler torpedoed the *City of Mandalay,* and Schultze sank the *Clan Chisholm.*

On the morning of October 18, Group Leader Hartmann reported to Wilhelmshaven that the hunting ought to be fine that day, but then up came British and French destroyers, which drove them under and harried them with depth charges, and in the afternoon a British Sunderland flying boat, which bombed them, and damaged the *U-48* so that Schultze had to turn homeward. Hartmann went on, however, and off Gibraltar sank three ships in rapid succession, the *Menin Ridge, Ledbury,* and *Tafna.*

On October 28, Hartmann reached the sea-lane of Cape Finisterre, but there found nothing. He was ordered to return to home waters. He came up and sank the Greek steamer *Trasyvoulos* on October 30. Then came a hard part of the journey, up around the Faroes, into the North Sea and back to Wilhelmshaven. He did not make port until November 12.

This was the first wolf pack, loose and not always under Dönitz's control. His orders were really confined to movement of the Hartmann group from one area to another, where the admiral knew the hunting would be good. But the principle was established beyond doubt. This was the way to sink ships out of convoys. All Admiral Dönitz needed was a much larger number of the Atlantic 500-ton U-boats.

Certainly if Dönitz had possessed those vessels just then, in the fall of 1940, he could have made life very much more difficult for the British than it was. The Royal Navy had only enough ships to convoy the merchantmen out past the western approaches to England; then the warships had to turn around and bring in other convoys that had made the crossing thus far. The middle of the Atlantic was a great open arena, covered neither by warships nor by aircraft, because the ships were too few and the aircraft did not have sufficient range. Thus, even though Admiral Dönitz was not yet able to put his wolf packs out to sea, he had good hunting for the individual U-boats, and early in the war this was made much better when the British codes were broken by B-Dienst, the secret radio intelligence section of the German admiralty. Fortunately for the British, with their shortage of escort vessels, Dönitz faced the same problem of shortages at the same time.

He was working on it. The promise he had wrung from Hitler made it possible to press for his plan of U-boat building once more. He would have only 64 U-boats at the end of December. If the navy followed his program, they would build 56 boats in 1940. In 1941 they would build 250 boats, more than 21 per month, and in 1942 they would build 29 boats per month. Theoretically, then, he would have 717 U-boats available by the end of 1942, and with this force, he should be able to bottle up England and cut her off from foreign shipping. The war would soon be over.

When Hitler saw this plan he howled. It would take all the Third Reich's naval resources to carry it out. The fact was that Hitler did not really appreciate the importance of the war against commerce. He was much more impressed with the sinking of a battleship or a carrier than with the sinking of a dozen shabby freighters. And so, when it came down to the fact, Dönitz did not get his ambitious building program, but something far, far less, a change that left him depressed and fretful. And yet it must be said for this thin-lipped, tough German admiral that he never let his own worries trouble the captains who fought for him so well. At Wilhelmshaven a great deal of effort was made to keep the morale of the U-boat force as high as the discipline. These were the two factors, above boats and armament, that could lead to victory.

2-2

2-1 Changing command. *U-9,* which has been sailed by Lieutenant Commander Hans-Joachim Schmidt-Weichert (right), now goes into the hands of Lieutenant Heinrich Klapdor. 2-2 The little 250-ton "canoe" *U-14* at sea. Lieutenant Wohlfahrt (left front in conning tower) took this little U-boat into the North Sea and sank four ships in the winter of 1939–40. 2-3 Lieutenant Klapdor on return from patrol. The beard was almost a necessity, given the shortage of hot water for shaving.

2-1

2-3

2-4

2-5

2-4 Skipper Klapdor of the *U-9* speaks to his deck crew before going out on patrol. 2-5 Practicing for aerial gunnery aboard *U-9*. It was not very serious practice—too many eyes on the camera. 2-6 *U-9* goes out on patrol. 2-7 Diving. 2-8 *U-9* returns from her first successful patrol.

2-6

2-7

2-8

2-9

2-10

2-11

2-12

2-9 The *U-48* in harbor in Norway. She returned to Germany safely on June 29, 1940. This was her sixth war patrol. Note black cat on conning tower. **2-10** The crew of the *U-48* take it easy on deck. **2-11** The *U-48*'s second skipper, Lieutenant Rösing. He survived his war patrols and was promoted to be commander of the 8th Flotilla at Kiel. **2-12** *U-48* crewmen take the sun. Left to right, Seamen Schmitz, Bohatzsch, and Wunderlich. **2-13** Mustering the crew for a ceremony.

2-13

2-14

2-15

2-14 *U-48* Bos'n's Mate Pohle emerges from the hatch. 2-15 Captain Herbert Schultze, *U-48*'s first skipper in the early months of the war, with Lieutenant Erich Zuern (with Iron Cross around his neck). Schultze was one of the most successful of all German U-boat captains and he later became commander of the U-boat flotilla at Lorient. 2-16 *U-48*'s Captain Herbert Schultze on a winter's day aboard the U-boat. 2-17 A little propaganda. In the spring of 1940 Hitler's troops raced through Belgium and by June France was defeated. This opened the whole western side of France to the U-boats, and they lost no time in moving to the Bay of Biscay.

2-17

2-18

2-19

2-18 The sinking of the *Royal Sceptre* by Herbert Schultze's *U-48* on September 5, 1939, brought a howl of protest from the British nearly as loud as that brought by the sinking of the liner *Athenia* just hours earlier (see text). **2-19** The *Royal Sceptre* lies sinking in the background, while part of the crew of the ship wave to the U-boat. Captain Schultze was cordiality itself to his victims; he gave them a bottle of whiskey and food and directions to the shore. **2-20** The return of the prize crew sent by the *U-48* to the *Leerdam.* After examining the ship and cargo, the *U-48* let this Dutch ship go. **2-21** But not this one. The SS *Heron's Pool,* just before the *U-48* put a torpedo into her. It is late afternoon of a gray Atlantic day.

2-21

2-24

2-22 Wilhelmshaven, 1940. The *U-44* (left) is tied up alongside the *U-52.* The former, with pennants flying, has just come back from a successful patrol. In the background is one of Germany's battleships. **2-23** The triumphal return of the *U-47* from Scapa Flow in October 1940, after the sinking of the British battleship HMS *Royal Oak,* inside Britain's fleet anchorage. It was one of Germany's great triumphs of the war. **2-24** With his leader, Lieutenant Commander Prien, the skipper of the *U-47*, is about to receive the Knight's Cross of the Iron Cross from Adolf Hitler, after his sinking of the HMS *Royal Oak.* **2-25** A proud Captain Dönitz inspects the crew of the *U-47* on their return from victory.

2-25

2-26

2-27

2-26 This is the *U-101* at sea. At left on the bridge is Captain Hans Rösing. At right is his First Watch Officer, Lieutenant Fritz Frauenheim. Both men won their *Ritterkreuz*. **2-27** Loading torpedoes at Kiel aboard the *U-40*. She was unlucky and ran into a mine in the Straits of Dover on October 13, 1939—much to the delight of Winston Churchill, who was becoming dispirited since the British had thus far sunk only three U-boats.

2-28   **2-29**

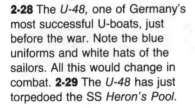

2-28 The *U-48,* one of Germany's most successful U-boats, just before the war. Note the blue uniforms and white hats of the sailors. All this would change in combat. **2-29** The *U-48* has just torpedoed the SS *Heron's Pool.*

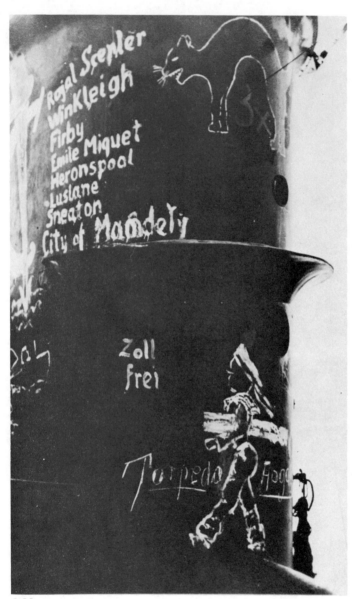

Royal Scepter
Winkleigh
Firby
Emile Miquet
Heronspool
Lustane
Sneaton
City of Mandely

Zoll
Frei

Torpedo Hoggo

2-30

2-30 When the *U-48* returned to port, her conning tower told the story of success. Each name represents a freighter sunk. **2-31** A buoy commemorating the *U-30,* a Type VII boat, Captain Lemp's famous boat which sank the liner *Athenia* in September 1939 and started the U-boat war on the wrong foot. The *U-30* survived the whole war and was scuttled in May 1945 by her crew. Lemp, who went on to the bigger and better boat *U-110,* was killed in 1941.

2-31

3. Nazis

By 1940 the U-bootwaffe had already begun to change in character. The prewar U-boat force was entirely made up of picked men. The officers who did the choosing were men like Captain Dönitz, still a figure in the tradition of the old Imperial German Navy. But as his experienced U-boat officers were killed and captured, and as it became necessary to expand the U-boat force, the Nazis began to move in. The difference was readily apparent in such boats as the *U-574*, whose skipper was Lieutenant Commander Meuhten.

Lieutenant Commander Meuhten was a sailor of the old school, a reserve officer who had served in U-boats in World War I, now called back to the colors to command a U-boat in the expansion program. He was a disciplinarian of the old school. Chief Petty Officer Weddikin recalled that the captain would not address a subordinate or allow himself to be addressed unless the subordinate kept a distance of three paces and stood at attention. Weddikin had to report to him that the deck crew was on parade in the morning, and ready for the first detail, scrubbing down the deck. The captain then came to the upper deck, Weddikin ordered the men to stop working and face the captain, and Weddikin stood smartly three paces away.

"Crew cleaning the upper deck, sir."

The skipper looked carefully and counted the paces.

"Aye, aye, carry on."

The skipper would never think of sitting down to table with an enlisted man. Indeed, one night during the Christmas season the men of the boat planned a little party and asked the captain to come. He never showed. But the first watch officer, Lieutenant Gengelbach, came. He was one of the new breed: he had come up through the Nazi ranks. As long as his men remained politically pure he was the soul of friendliness.

Soon, the *U-574* had a new skipper, Lieutenant Veihinger, another Nazi, twenty-seven years old.

In the early days of 1939 and 1940 the U-boat skippers were men of the old school. But it changed in a year.

The British were to see more Nazis, many more. Lieutenant Hans Jenisch's *U-32* was attacked on her eighth war cruise in October 1940, and sunk by scuttling. When British naval intelligence men interrogated the prisoners of war from the *U-32*, they found that "they are all fanatical Nazis and hate the British intensely, an attitude which has not been so evident in previous cases."

Jenisch's men were a real eye-opener to the British, for they seemed to hate their skipper as much as they did the enemy. Perhaps it was because he was not a Nazi.

"They are advocates of unrestricted warfare and are prepared to condone all aggressive violence, cruelty, breaches of treaties, and other crimes as being necessary to the rise of the German race to the control of Europe."

Some captains were tough just to be tough, like Prien, who had a good deal of the Nazi in him. He was cordially hated by his crew. One day he came on deck and spotted an enemy aircraft before the lookout sang out. The lookout got five days' detention, to be served on their next leave. At one point morale was so bad aboard Prien's boat that the petty officers went to Dönitz. Two-thirds of the deck hands, they told the commander, had punishment tours to serve when the boat docked after patrol. Dönitz did not like that. He reprimanded Prien, and changed the whole crew. Not one man of the old crew went back aboard the *U-47*.

Schepke was another who had a Nazi crew, and he was good to them. After the capture of his boat in 1941, however, British intelligence noted with disgust that they had never seen "such a lot of nasty little Nazis" as came off the Schepke boat into captivity.

The Nazi leaders of the Third Reich did everything they could to lionize their U-boat skippers, for Dr. Josef Goebbels saw the immense value of the publicity they could bring Germany among neutral nations who like heroes in any war. War correspondents were often assigned to submarines, such as Prien's *U-47* and Kretschmer's *U-99*. Altogether, the naval branch of the propaganda ministry numbered some 3,000 men under Wolfgang Frank (who had accompanied several U-boats on cruises and later was to make a postwar reputation as a chronicler of U-boat history). The U-boat section included about a dozen "war correspondents" who went out with the boats and then wrote stirring stories about the German victories. One of these Nazi propagandists was Helmut Ecke, who carried the rank of temporary sub-lieutenant. He had come to the propagandists by way of the Berlin newspaper *Berliner Zeitung am Mittag,* and he was a grand figure with a car and driver. In May 1941 he set out with skipper Julius Lemp in the *U-110* for what was supposed to be a historic and highly publicized cruise. At one point the *U-110* stopped and Lemp conferred with Captain Schnee, skipper of the *U-32.* They planned an attack on a convoy, and journalist Ecke filmed it all for the German newsreels, and later releases to neutral countries. It was to be part of an epic story about Lemp, one of Admiral Dönitz's aces. But the best-laid plans of the propagandists did sometimes go astray and this was one time. Lemp's boat was sunk, and Ecke lost all his cameras and all his films, although his life was saved so that he could go into prison camp and spend the rest of the war contemplating the "great victories" coming undone.

Fritz-Julius Lemp, the man who set the tone of the U-boat war with the sinking of the *Athenia,* did not survive the sinking of his *U-110.*

His crew represented the dichotomy of the old and new Germany. Lemp himself was of the old: he had been born at Tsingtao, the capital of the German China colony of Kiaochao, in 1913, the son of a Prussian army officer, and had entered the navy in 1931, long before the coming of the Nazis. He had been very popular with his crew.

It so happened that Lemp's first watch officer was his cousin. So happened? Probably not. Probably Lemp had yielded to the impulse of the Prussian military class, to pave the way for this relative. If so, he must have realized before the end that he had made a dreadful mistake, because his cousin, Lieutenant Löwe, was everything that Lemp was not: a boor, a Nazi, an overbearing and churlish officer.

"He was," said the British Naval Intelligence officer who questioned Löwe, "narrow-minded, callous, brutal and a bully, as well as intolerant of any criticism of the regime, which he ardently supported. He might be taken as one of the fine flowers of Nazism."

The crew detested Löwe.

The second watch officer, Lieutenant Ulrich Wehrhrofer, was a genial fellow, bumbling and grinning, but at least no Nazi. He told the British without much halting that he thought the Nazis were quite dreadful.

The engineer officer was Lieutenant Hans-Joachim Eichelborn, not a Nazi, but an admirer of Hitler for what he had done for Germany. He called himself a German patriot. So did one of the petty officers, a man who had served for a long time in the merchant service of Germany. He had spent many months in one of the Nazis' concentration camps. He was fighting for Germany, he said, and not the Nazis.

Every month the Nazis made greater inroads into the U-boat service, and it would not be long before they forced Dönitz to accept "political officers" aboard the U-boats in exchange for the Nazi regime's promotion of the U-boat service so that Dönitz would have the manning he needed. This politicization of the U-boat service did nothing to help its efficiency. The crews were divided; anti-Nazis had to whisper among themselves and watch the Nazis who would turn them in for antigovernment activity at the drop of a watch cap. Again, the dichotomy was apparent between old and new, as with Lieutenant Commander Gert Schreiber's *U-95*.

Schreiber was born in Silesia in 1912 and joined the German navy in the old days. He was of the same class as Prien and Lemp in the officer corps. She was sunk in the fall of 1941 in the Mediterranean by the Dutch submarine O-21. Only twelve Germans survived: among them were skipper Schreiber, an officer of the old sort; his first lieutenant, a rigid Nazi bloodthirstily predicting the almost immediate invasion and conquest of England; and a junior officer who had somehow transferred from the Luftwaffe to the U-boat service—a patriot, not a Nazi, who had already made 110 war missions in aircraft. The fourth officer to survive was a Viennese yachtsman. The two surviving petty officers were both old navy men. But the crew, most of whom had drowned, were youngsters, a mixed bag of Hitler Youth and draftees.

The difficulties of the U-boat arm grew worse and worse as the propaganda campaign continued to build up the U-boat force in the face of growing difficulties. The capture of *U-570* without a struggle indicated something new. When British intelligence traced the story, they learned that although the first watch officer was a Nazi, the second watch officer was not a Nazi and not very friendly to Nazism, the engineer officer was

a professional sailor, and so were most of the petty officers. The youngsters of the crew had been Nazis, but when the fabric of their world
collapsed it did not take long for their political beliefs to change.

"The impression gained was that propaganda had built up the morale
of the crew to a high level. What had been built was upon sand and
when the storm arose it fell and great was the fall of it. After their ready
surrender the crew forgot both the glamour of the U-boat service and
the perils of submarine warfare and in a somewhat childish way turned
to consider the more domestic problems of their life as prisoners. They
seem to have shed their Nazism more easily than most prisoners."

3-1 A ship launching attracted all types, from stern naval officers to the paunchy Nazis on right. Note the absence of Nazi salutes from the navy..

3-1

3-2

3-2 A rare photo of Hitler
with his U-boat officers—rare
because Hitler really did not like
the navy, and because the austere,
confident Dönitz seemed to
intimidate him.

4. Uncertain Winter

The year 1940 opened dismally. The weather in the North Sea and the North Atlantic, of course, was its usual stormy self, but both Englishmen and Germans had been used to that for a thousand years and more. Geography did play an important part in the U-boat war, however, this winter. A look at the map of Northern Europe shows why: maritime Germany is split in two. Kiel, the great naval base, faces on the Baltic Sea. German ships wishing to move into the Atlantic from Kiel had to pass between the Danish and Swedish coasts, then up through the Kattegat and the Skagerrak, two large bodies of water that were in reality small seas, and thence out into the North Sea off the southern coast of Norway. The alternative route, built for the Kaiser's navy before World War I, was through the Kiel Canal across the Schleswig-Holstein peninsula, into the North Sea just northwest of Hamburg. It was not only inconvenient, but could be dangerous for U-boats, because not all the Swedes and Danes and Norwegians were neutral: the British had many supporters and watchers on the shores. U-boats using the northern route were much at risk all the time they worked in these narrow waters. There were other naval bases—Wilhelmshaven, for example—but once again the difficulties were serious, and the advantage of the British and the French was obvious. One help had been the creation of a large submarine facility on the rock called Heligoland, well out into the North Sea, but Heligoland was nothing more than rock, it did not even have a ship harbor, and the submarine haven had been built by blasting holes in the flat western sections. The U-boat men faced the exigencies of a Northern European winter. The stormy weather slowed down the sea war, and that month the mines sowed by the little 250-ton submarines sank more ships than did the big oceangoing U-boats—by thirty-three to twenty-five.

That was not to say that the U-boats were not out, as much and as far as they could get. In the early days of January, Lieutenant Kuppisch's *U-58* sank two ships, keeping Kuppisch's name right up there among the most successful of Germany's U-boat captains. But success was not always easy to find. Lieutenant Schepke set out on patrol, and on January 8 was off the Humber River estuary of England. Near midnight a steamer was sighted, and sunk by torpedo. This was the Norwegian steamer *Manx*. Immediately, one of the patrol destroyers in the area was pouncing on the *U-19*, and drove her under the water, then began a long siege of depth-charging. The *U-19* was damaged and hit the bottom. Repairs were made, but when Skipper Schepke tried to bring the boat up, she would not respond. The rudders had been damaged and on the bottom there was not much to be done about that. The only way to get her up was to blow ballast and use the electric motors as rudders, which took a great deal of patience and skill. Finally this was done, the valves were opened, fresh air was blown into the boat, and the port diesel was hooked to the electric engines to charge them up. They were saved, and young Schepke, then just a junior lieutenant with his first command, was preserved to become one of Germany's "aces."

On January 11, Lieutenant Otto Kretschmer was poking around the Shetlands in his little *U-23*. Among other things he reported back to Dönitz that the British had deserted Scapa Flow as their fleet base, which was perfectly true. Not until much later, when the security of Scapa could be guaranteed, would Churchill move the fleet back there.

Kretschmer was indefatigably curious and aggressive. He continued poking around the little bays of the northland. In one of them, "Inganes Bay" on the German chart, lay a tanker at anchor. Through the periscope, Kretschmer took several long looks, and estimated his chances. Nearly any other skipper would have passed this one by. The crooked channel made it impossible to shoot from outside. The bay was very narrow, the entrance tiny, the turning room inside almost nonexistent. If that was not enough to discourage Kretschmer, he also saw two destroyers anchored near the tanker. The only possible way to do it was to go in on the surface at high speed, fire at the tanker, and then turn and run for the sea before the anchored destroyers could get moving. On the surface? The conventional torpedo attack was made while submerged, but that would never do in this case. So on the surface it would be. Kretschmer steamed in boldly, fired, hit the Danish tanker *Danmark* amidships, and her cargo of gasoline blew to the skies. The destroyermen were quick to their posts, but they scarcely saw the little U-boat as it sped out and down into the safety of the North Sea. Kretschmer had invented a new U-boat tactic, the high-speed surface strike. It was a new strategy for the captains to think about. So was the exploit of Lieutenant Wolfgang Lüth: on the night of January 18, off the east coast of Scotland, Lüth's *U-9* sank the Swedish steamer *Flandria,* and an hour later the Swedish *Patria.* The accomplishments of these little boats, which the U-boat men called "canoes," were far greater than anyone had expected before the war. For example, late in the fall the battleship HMS *Nelson,* flagship of the British home fleet, had run into one of those mines laid by a "canoe" in Loch Ewe, and was laid up for many weeks.

As can be seen in the above, by this time, four months after the beginning of hostilities, the "rules of war" concerning submarines were in tatters. The most unfortunate victims were the neutral ships moving in the North Sea and North Atlantic. If the Swedes and Norwegians and Danes wished to ship to the rest of the world (barring the Baltic states) they had to round the coast of the British Isles and go out into the Atlantic. That put them under the eyes of the U-boats coming and going, and in the cold weather of this winter, the U-boats took less and less care to make sure that the ships at which they were firing were enemy ships, or even neutral ships carrying enemy cargo. By this time, frankly, the U-boat men considered just about everybody on the high seas their enemies and were willing to fire first and ask questions later. Germany was also moving toward such an official policy, with a constant barrage of world propaganda against the neutrals. In fact, a very large number of Swedish and Norwegian ship-owners were carrying products destined for Britain or its empire. Several Swedish and Norwegian vessels were sunk in this period, as the U-boat captains paid less attention to the troublesome rules.

By the first of the year 1940 it became apparent in political circles in Germany and Britain that a crisis was approaching in Scandinavia. The Danes, who shared a common border with Germany, had long accepted the necessity of getting along with their big neighbor. The Swedes maintained a studied neutrality. But the Norwegians were very much split in their feelings, and most of the seafarers leaned toward England. Since autumn the British had been paying special attention to shipping across the North Sea, for as the war progressed it became apparent that the iron ore of Norway was a prize for which Britain and Germany would contest. At the moment Norway was shipping to both sides. Winston Churchill advocated the immediate invasion of Norway, but he was lord of the admiralty, not prime minister, and he was over-ruled. Well, if he could not achieve his ends in one way, he would try in another. He ordered the organization of convoys to bring the precious Norwegian iron ore to Britain. It was on the first of these convoys that the escorting destroyer *Daring* was sunk by Kretschmer. With that sinking, Kretschmer joined an exclusive club within Dönitz's U-bootwaffe, that select list of captains who had sunk an enemy warship.

At that point, just before the spring of 1940, the efforts of the U-boat captains were recognized by Dönitz and that was really enough. Only two of those captains had been awarded the famous *Ritterkreuz,* the Knight's Cross of the Iron Cross. Lieutenant Prien was one, famous in Germany for his remarkable exploit in sinking the *Royal Oak.* The other was Lieutenant Herbert Schulze, who was doing precisely what Dönitz wanted, concentrating on the sinking of enemy merchant ships to try to starve Britain out of the war.

At the beginning of March 1940, Admiral Dönitz assessed his situation. He had three types of U-boats in operation, the 250-ton Type II, the 500-ton Type VII, and the 740-ton Type IX. All were proving themselves, the small boats for minelaying and North Sea operations, the Type VIIs for war in the mid-Atlantic, and the Type IXs to cross the Atlantic and attack the British supply lines at the dispatch end. But the number of U-boats available to Dönitz for operations was at a low point. He expected improvement with new boats coming out of production. But he had not counted on Hitler's plans. On March 4, 1940, Dönitz's concentration on the shipping lanes was interrupted by orders from naval headquarters: All further sailings of U-boats were to be stopped. U-boats at sea would stay away from the Norwegian coast. All U-boats would be made ready for operations and held.

Dönitz hurried up to Berlin that night to protest. Next day he was told what was going to happen.

Hitler had ordered the occupation of Denmark and Norway. Dönitz was to be ready by March 10 to protect German naval and transport forces in the North Sea. Commerce raiding had to stop, while the U-boats were turned to purely military matters.

So short was Dönitz of boats that he had to discontinue his training program at the submarine school. Using every boat, he would have nineteen 250-ton boats, and twelve oceangoing boats. The battle for Norway was about to begin.

4-1 The fate of so many ships in this war at sea. Her boilers blowing steam, a British freighter goes down after being torpedoed in mid-Atlantic. **4-2** The perennial problem. A U-boat man cartoonist makes light of the difficulties of coping with the underwater plumbing of a submarine. The disembodied voice of a crewman in distress behind the door calls in the repairman to "hurry up" while he who works the pump tells him to "shut up."

4-1

4-2

4-3 The U-boat tender *Saar.* **4-4** Christmas Party 1939. Plenty of wine and beer tonight, but tomorrow? Most of these young men will not survive the war at sea.

4-5

4-5 Crewmen in port carry shells to stow below. These are for the 10.5-centimeter gun, approximately equivalent to the U.S. 6-inch gun. **4-6** Commander Wolfgang Lüth of the *U-43* with his *Ritterkreuz* (Knight's Cross of the Iron Cross).

4-6

4-7

4-8

4-9

4-10

4-7 The *U-43* in the Kaiser Wilhelm Kanal (Kiel Canal). The temperature is 16 degrees Fahrenheit. **4-8** The *U-46* alongside the submarine tender *Acheron.* Like the *U-48,* the *U-46* survived the entire war, and was scuttled in Wilhelmshaven at the end. **4-9** In the Kiel Canal. The *U-48* passes beneath the Rendsburger Hochbrücke. **4-10** The *U-48* moves out from Heligoland base behind the icebreaker.

4-11

4-12

4-11 Two crewmen of the little *U-18*. The beards say they have been at sea for a week. At left is Obermaschinist Benzinger, and at right Obersteuerman Thieme. Many years later the latter became an admiral in the East German navy. **4-12** The *U-433* with Captain Hans Ey at the compass. Behind him a lookout scans the horizon. Despite all the care, the *U-433* was sunk south of Malaga in November 1941. **4-13** The *U-70* at sea, preparing to drop anchor. A Type II boat, she was sunk off Ireland in March 1941 by a British corvette.

4-13

5. The Atlantic War

Until the spring of 1940, Hitler had hoped that he could achieve his aims without much more fighting on the western front. He would dearly have liked to have brought that war to an end by reaching some accommodation with the British and the French, for his real interest was in driving east.

But the British had shown no interest in accommodating him. They saw the war as a real and permanent state of affairs until Hitler was defeated. The British plan for movement into Norway, engineered by Winston Churchill and finally accepted by the War Cabinet, was the evidence of it. At sea, the British were also showing their belligerence. They had cost Dönitz eight submarines by March 1940.

The struggle for Norway came in April. The Germans really had the advantage; they moved troops easily by land into Denmark, and from there up north. But the British interest in Norway was in the northern sector, around Narvik, where the orefields lay. Both sides had to approach this area from the sea. In the sea fighting that followed, the German submarines were of very little use. The water was too shallow, their mission was too narrow (to protect the invading forces, as they were told); as Dönitz could have informed Admiral Raeder, had he been asked, the submarine, although an admirable offensive device, was not a good defensive weapon. But worst of all, Dönitz that spring became aware of a dreadful deficiency in his force. His torpedoes were not working.

For months the captains had been coming back to port to report on "misses." As was always the case, the staff regarded most of these reports as alibis and defended the torpedoes. For example, on October 30, *U-56* reported that she had tracked a British naval convoy, which included the battleships *Rodney* and *Nelson* and the battle cruiser *Hood,* and had fired three torpedoes and scored hits on the battleships, but that none of the torpedoes had exploded.

Sure, said U-boat command. Sure. And the staff put it down to another alibi by a poor shot of a captain.

But by the spring of 1940 Admiral Dönitz was not so sure. Prien, Schultze, and other respected skippers were coming home with the same sort of tales. You couldn't fight a war with a blunted sword, Prien said bitterly when he came back from one patrol that was a spectacular failure, although he had fired at half a dozen ships.

And then came Norway. Prien went on patrol, found a whole lane of British transports lying off Bygdenfjord, fired eight torpedoes, and none of them exploded. Other U-boats made four attacks on the battleship *Warspite,* fourteen attacks on one cruiser, ten on one destroyer, and more on transports, with the complete result: one transport sunk.

The torpedo the U-boats were then carrying had been developed between the wars. It depended on a magnetic device to explode it electronically when it came within the magnetic influence of a ship's bottom. It was a wonderful idea: a skipper did not actually have to hit a ship, but only to come near it, for the torpedo to explode and tear a hole in the hull. But the magnetic torpedoes were not working. And the captains discovered that the depth settings on the torpedoes were not working either, so that, when they cut off the magnetic factor, they found they were shooting underneath their targets.

The morale of the U-boat force slipped to zero. It could not slip any more even when the U-boats were detailed to act as transports and carry munitions to Trondheim. Captains like Prien were wondering why they had ever gotten into the U-boat service.

Dönitz was convinced that the torpedoes were at fault, and he did the only thing he could; he ordered all magnetic exploders disconnected. Still, too often the torpedoes did not go off. Or they exploded prematurely.

The final answer, in the middle of the Norwegian campaign, was to withdraw all the U-boats, a matter that hurt the U-boat service enormously in the eyes of Adolf Hitler. Had he depended on the U-boat to win in Norway he would have lost; they were of virtually no help at all, and he did not forget it.

So April ended with a torpedo commission trying to figure out what was wrong with the main weapon of the U-boats, and the U-boats lying idle in port, and the crews wishing they were in the Luftwaffe or anywhere else. In a few months the torpedo experts were disgraced, and tried and convicted of dereliction of duty and other offenses, but that did not solve the problem. Precious weeks went by, and the British enjoyed a virtual holiday from submarine attack. Sinkings fell from the 100,000 to 200,000 tons per month of the past to 47,000 tons in March, 31,000 tons in April, and 48,000 tons in May.

These months tried Admiral Dönitz and the U-boat corps. The admiral went from base to base, explaining the torpedo problem and what was being done to correct it. Finally, when he felt that he had a weapon that could sink ships, he decided to send out a captain. He had to send someone he trusted implicitly, and he sent Lieutenant Viktor Öhrn in *U-37,* to show what a 500-ton Atlantic boat could do with the changed torpedoes. Öhrn sailed from Wilhelmshaven on May 15 and returned on June 9 with flags flying, and pennants representing 47,000 tons of enemy shipping. Öhrn's single submarine had sunk as much in three weeks as had the whole U-boat corps in March! Morale took a surge and captains were pleading for assignments. The crisis for the U-boat force was over.

Meanwhile, Hitler's land forces were bringing another major change in the war that would revolutionize Admiral Dönitz's operations. The "Sitzkrieg" in the west ended with the Norway invasion. The Wehrmacht staged a lightning strike through Belgium in the six weeks between May 10 and June 25; the Germans defeated the combined French and British armies in the west, brought about the fall of the French government, France's withdrawal from the war, and, above all, the occupation of northern and western France. Suddenly, the U-boats had a whole new scene of operation. No longer did they have to go through the North Sea to round Scotland and get into the Atlantic. Suddenly all of France, all those ports from Dunkirk to Hendaye, belonged to the U-boats. Dönitz saw immediately that Brest and Lorient would make admirable bases. On June 23, even before the struggle ended officially, he flew in a Junkers transport to Lorient. And there he gazed across the water. Here would be the center of U-boat activity for the future. The officers would be housed in the hotels of this port. The men would get the lesser hostelries and the City Music Academy. In Kerneval, he would establish his own administrative headquarters, with the best of communications.

For now, with bases at Kiel and Wilhelmshaven and the red rock of Heligoland and France, his radio direction-finding system was to be vastly improved, and that meant faster service in discovering the enemy at sea through radio transmissions. As for the U-boats themselves, all they had to do was sail straight out from the ports into the Atlantic and the Bay of Biscay, and they were at the throats of their enemies.

New names came into the vocabularies of the U-boat men. Lorient, La Pallice, St. Nazaire, La Rochelle—these were to be the new submarine bases. Admiral Dönitz saw his chance to score heavily against the British and he was determined to take it. He also knew of the plans developing in the German high command for an invasion of England that summer or fall. All that was necessary was the "softening up," which Luftwaffe chief Hermann Göring promised to do that summer. Dönitz was to be involved by sinking ever more British ships and thus making Churchill's supply problems impossible. Dönitz was well aware of the value he could get from cooperation between U-boat and aircraft, but this summer, with Göring's mind almost totally confined to the air war against Britain, he could not expect much.

The performance of his captains put the problem at least temporarily out of the admiral's mind.

"We have seized the English by their throats," boasted the Goebbels propaganda. Every day the radio reported new victories at sea: five freighters sunk on September 10, eleven freighters torpedoed on the night of September 21. . . . Dönitz orchestrated the whole effort with his grid map and his high-speed radio transmitters, and the sinkings came day after day. He wanted at least a sinking a day to aid the propaganda campaign and to restore the U-boat arm in the eyes of the high command. He very nearly got it. In June the U-boats sank 260,000 tons of ships and that was a figure to shoot at from that point on.

New names began to join the list of lion-captains: Otto Kretschmer, Werner Hartmann, Hans Rösing, Fritz Frauenheim, Engelbert Endrass, Heinrich Kuhnke, Joachim Schepke, Hans Jenisch, Heinrich Bleichrodt, Viktor Öhrn, Wolfgang Lüth. Before the end of autumn all these men had joined Prien and Schultze as holders of the coveted Knight's Cross of the Iron Cross, and Prien held the cross with oak leaves. Generally speaking, the Knight's Cross came with the sinking of 100,000 tons of shipping, or some heroic venture against the enemy warships, such as Prien's. In Germany these heroes were known to every schoolboy, but the U-boat arm was just beginning to get international notoriety. In the fall of 1940, the British still did not know Kretschmer's first name, and they misspelled Schuhart's. They would learn.

So eager was Dönitz to keep his boats at sea that when a captain and crew came in for rest, their boat might go out again under another skipper while they went home on leave. Thus it was in May that the *U-48* went out not with Lieutenant Commander Herbert Schultze on the bridge, but Lieutenant Commander Hans-Rudolf Rösing. The Germans had a different manning system than the British and Americans. As in all navies, the skipper was almost all-powerful. In the German U-boat navy, he *was* the U-boat. Also, in the American and British navies, his second in command was an executive officer, whereas in the German submarine service the officers other than engineering were called watch officers. First watch officer aboard the *U-48* on this patrol was Lieutenant Reinhard Suhren, just beginning a distinguished career as a submariner.

They sailed off from the Tirpitz mole in Kiel on May 26. They had to put in at Trondheim in Norway for some repairs, but by June 3 they were on the high sea and sinking enemy ships. On the morning of June 6, they sank the steamer *Stancor* with the deck gun (77 shots), which gave rise to a new order by Dönitz that the weapon of sinking was the torpedo. Well, they could do that too, and the next day they sank the steamer *Frances Massey*. They sank the steamer *Eros,* and the *Violanda N. Goulandris.*

U-43 found a convoy, and Dönitz sent the *U-29, U-46, U-48,* and *U-101* to attack together. They sank three freighters in the convoy. Before the war patrol ended, the *U-48* had sunk 42,000 tons of ships, and then returned to Kiel in triumph. This was the sort of work that Dönitz appreciated. A job marked by brilliant and tenacious ferocity in attack, said the commander of U-boats when his boys came home.

In July the Germans began to make really good use of Lorient, southeast of Brest. At first it was just a staging base. How could it be much else, so soon after the defeat of France? The U-boats pulled in there to top off their fuel, after having gone around from Germany, and then they went out again. For practical purposes, the new base extended the submarine's range by 450 miles. At the end of the patrol, if they were in the vicinity, they dropped by Lorient to pick up more fuel and then went back to Germany. To the crews, this was an eminently satisfactory arrangement, but to Dönitz it was not. The long trip to Germany, either through the English Channel or up around Scotland, was extremely dangerous and became more so every month as Britain increased her number of escorts and aircraft. By the first of July 1940, Dönitz had lost twenty-three U-boats in this war, and that was not satisfactory at all. Much danger could be eliminated by basing the crews in the French ports, allowing them home leave only every year or so, and then bringing them home by air or train. The U-boats would stay in France.

So the buildup of the French U-boat ports began. It was not long before Allied observation planes began to notice the changes. More ships, cranes, and port facilities were brought in, and back in Germany Dönitz began the planning that would make Lorient the forward naval command base of the U-boat force. He looked to the days when the enemy might have much stronger air forces than they had in 1940, and began plans for bomb-proof submarine pens in the conquered territories.

The wolf-pack concept was never far from Dönitz's mind. His admirable grid system and good communications made it possible to keep tight control of the U-boats at sea. That summer of 1940 he had another stroke of good fortune when the Germans broke the British merchant shipping codes, and then could "read the enemy's mail." By September it was all set, and a convoy was selected for a new wolf-pack attack. SC 2 was the name of the convoy, heading from Canada to England with fifty-one ships full of war materials. Dönitz planned to intercept the convoy in the wide belt of unprotected sea, around 19 degrees west longitude. The U-boats were there, at the right place at the right time, and they took four ships out of the convoy in a hurry. Two days later they took two ships from another convoy, and three days after that another four ships from a third convoy.

A very important change was added to the wolf-pack technique that summer by Otto Kretschmer. As a reward for his excellent service in the North Sea, Dönitz had given Kretschmer command of the *U-99*,* a brand-new 500-ton Atlantic Type VII boat. Kretschmer did not disappoint his commanding officer, and neither did the other young skippers. In the month of September they sank almost 300,000 tons of shipping.

---

*Very shortly after the outbreak of war, Dönitz realized that it was playing into the hands of the enemy to number his U-boats serially. So the numbers began to mount, much faster than the number of U-boats. By war's end the boats were up in the 3500s, although in total only about 900 U-boat keels were ever laid.

That late summer, the U-boats represented a great opportunity for German propaganda, to hide the fact that Göring's attempt to break Britain's air defenses had failed. On August 15, in the culmination of a fierce series of air battles over Britain, 180 German planes were shot down. At this point even Göring had to admit that he could not guarantee the success of Operation Sea Lion, the proposed amphibious invasion of England, and the invasion was tabled. The Luftwaffe then turned to a punishing technique. Night after night for months they would send bombers over Britain to destroy anything and everything. They were attacking, in reality, British morale. At this point, the U-boat successes were very useful to Dr. Goebbels's propaganda efforts; they helped hide the fact that for the first time, at the English Channel and in the air, the indomitable German war machine had been stopped cold.

Hitler noticed. Hitler had never cared much for the U-boats, did not much like Dönitz, and still resented the pressure the latter had put on him at the hero ceremonies for Lieutenant Prien. But against the failure of Göring's Luftwaffe, the U-boat successes stood like a beacon, and the Führer had to take notice of them. He was persuaded (reluctantly) that the total blockade of Britain was necessary to the success of the war. He thus legitimized what Dönitz had been doing already, sinking neutral ships in British waters. The danger of bringing America into the war was increased, but the failure of Göring meant that there could be no short war, with German troops strolling up Pall Mall that fall. The war was going to be long and hard, and the way to victory, Dönitz said, was to starve the British out. So be it. That was the new German policy for the war at sea.

Now the new bases in France were doubled and redoubled: at La Pallice, Brest, Saint-Nazaire, and in the ports of Norway, new bases with submarine pens were built. Dönitz was knuckling down for a long, hard war.

At that time, in the summer of 1940, Dönitz still had only about thirty oceangoing boats to command, and half of these were always laid up for one reason or another. He was lucky if he could keep ten boats fighting at the same time. Then, that fall, along came Otto Kretschmer with a new technique; the night-convoy *surface* attack.

For years the U-boat men had operated within crafts with split personalities. The U-boats—and all other "submarines" of the times—were not actually submarines at all but submersibles. Their greatest speed was attained on the surface. Any prolonged activity underwater was uncomfortable and downright dangerous at a point, because of the buildup of gases and pressure. And yet, the deep was their element, the deep where they could skulk and sneak and find their prey, then approach him and blow him out of the water without ever being seen.

As Kretschmer had deduced, however, the convoy offered an opportunity for a new sort of attack. The usual convoy consisted of columns of ships, kept well apart to prevent collisions. Outside, the convoy escorts roamed around, looking for signs of submarines.

The trick would be to get *inside* the convoy, fire, run, and get out, then perhaps get in again, or if necessary submerge and hide from the enemy escort vessels. Inside the convoy, a captain could simply fire a fan spread of torpedoes, with a very good chance of hitting something.

It could not be done, said the British.

It could be done, said Otto Kretschmer.

On the night of October 18 Kretschmer set out to prove his theory. Dönitz had directed him to Convoy SC 7 along with Liebe's *U-38*. That night, Kretschmer took his *U-99 inside* the convoy and in rapid succession sank four ships. Men aboard other ships of the convoy saw the submarine, on the surface, moving alongside. Then, long before dawn, the submarine went down, out of the convoy, and escaped.

When the British heard the reports from the merchant seamen, at first the high officials of the navy refused to believe it. A submarine inside the convoy? Nonsense. It was too dangerous. But Kretschmer's technique was swiftly copied by Prien and others, and Convoy HX 79 lost fourteen ships to a wolf pack operating in and out of the convoy mostly on the surface.

Otto Kretschmer had added another page to naval strategy and to history.

5-1

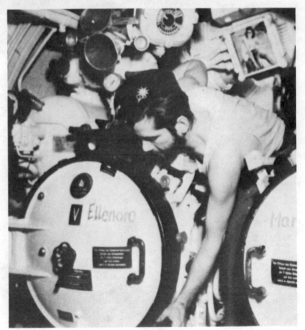

5-2

5-1 The deck officers of *U-96* beginning their second year of war. Left to right, Lieutenant Horst Hamm, Captain Heinrich Lehmann-Willenbrock, Lieutenant Friedrich Grade, and Lieutenant Harde Rodler von Roithberg. This Type VII U-boat was to give a good account of herself in the Battle of the Atlantic, until one day in the spring of 1945 when she was sunk in Wilhelmshaven harbor by an American army bomber. These officers were long gone from the boat by then, and most of them were dead. Von Roithberg, skipper of the *U-989,* went down with all his men on Valentine's Day 1945, sunk by British escorts in the North Atlantic. **5-2** A torpedoman aboard *U-124* checking his tubes. Note the profusion of dials and crowded equipment and the picture of the pretty girl above the torpedoman's back. The tubes, also, were named for girl friends.

5-3

5-4

5-5

5-3 On watch on a dirty day in the North Atlantic. **5-4** Storing provisions at Lorient for the voyage outside. When the U-boats went out, they were jammed with fresh food, but that was gone soon enough, and after two weeks they were eating out of cans. The food was sometimes very good and sometimes very bad. "The worst I ever ate," recalled an old U-boat man forty years later. But one thing was certain, a really bad cook never lasted aboard past his first voyage. **5-5** A U-boat drydock. **5-6** The torpedoes went out bearing little messages, painted on by the torpedomen. The one in the middle with the shark says, "My Watchword: Destruction!"

5-6

5-7 "Mother" Rosiefski, the foster mother to all the U-boat men. She ran a coffee house in Bremen. Her necklace is studded with models of all the U-boats which she had adopted. 5-8 Admiral Dönitz and Grand Admiral Raeder, first row. Behind them are Commander Kuhnke and (right) Lieutenant Commander von Bülow, both heroes of the U-boat world. 5-9 U-boat tender *Waldemar Kophamel* at sea. 5-10 Building the pens at Lorient. The Todt Organization, Germany's best engineering group, was told what Dönitz wanted and they produced it: bomb-proof bunkers for the U-boats. At this stage of the construction the bunkers were very vulnerable, and bombing by the RAF would have destroyed the structures; constant bombing would have made it impossible to build them. But for reasons the Germans never understood (but were thankful for) the RAF did not bother them at all. So in the end, Dönitz got his bomb-proof shelters.

5-11

5-12

5-11 A completed U-boat bunker. Once these were in place, the U-boats were completely safe as long as they did not venture out to sea. **5-12** Lager Lemp, Lorient. This rest camp (named after Skipper Lemp's death) was a haven in the summer for the tired U-boat sailors. In the winter it was better to be in town . . . until the saturation bombings began in 1944. **5-13** These are the bunkers at Saint-Nazaire under construction. **5-14** Part of the crew of the *U-25* at Kiel. She was a Type I-A boat, one of only two built during the war years.

5-14

5-15 The *U-25*'s impressive conning tower with the deck gun on right. **5-16** The *U-25* loading torpedoes at Kiel. The torpedoes looked deadly enough, but during the battle for Norway Dönitz discovered that he had more than his share of duds, and the U-boat force nearly came unraveled because of it (see text). **5-17** The victim in the background, the assassin (*U-25*) in midground, taken from the *U-43* on July 1, 1940. A month later the *U-25* was sunk in the North Sea by a mine.

5-15

5-16

5-17

5-18

5-19

5-20

5-18 The *U-37* moving into the new base at Lorient, France, in August 1940, after the fall of France. **5-19** Happy to be back. The crew of the *U-37* listen to the band welcoming them back to Lorient. **5-20** Washup. The men of *U-37* do a little washing up at Lorient, before going ashore.

5-21 The *U-37* sinks the freighter *Samala,* September 1940. **5-22** The lifeboats of the freighter *Samala* in calm seas. **5-23** The captain of the *U-37,* Lieutenant Commander Victor Öhrn, on the bridge as the boat enters Lorient. After the torpedo troubles, most of Dönitz's captains were completely dispirited. Öhrn went out in the summer of 1940 with redesigned torpedoes, and sank nearly 50,000 tons of shipping all by himself. The effect on the U-boat force was instantaneous and positive. **5-24** Pleased as punch. When Victor Öhrn returned with his big bag of ships to Lorient in 1940 he was greeted by a jubilant Admiral Dönitz.

5-22

5-25

5-25 Günther Prien's *U-47* has just sunk the Portuguese freighter *Gonzalo Nelho* and the U-boat is now picking up the lifeboat to interrogate the survivors. **5-26** Prien, of the *U-47*, center with binoculars, was easily the most celebrated of the U-boat captains in these early days.

5-26

6. The Wolf Packs

The year 1941 was the year of the wolf pack. Circumstances combined to make the German strategy extremely successful against Great Britain. The principal advantage Dönitz held at this point was still the Atlantic's great size. Even after the occupation of Iceland by the British and the establishment of destroyer and air bases, there continued to be a large section of ocean through which the convoys had to pass with very little protection. It was in the mid-Atlantic area that the German U-boat wolf packs did their deadly work most effectively.

In this winter of 1941, Admiral Dönitz was in Lorient, with Chief of Staff Godt and his entire entourage. Their *Lagezimmer*—situation room—was the heart of the U-boat operation system. Night and day the situation room was manned, as were the communications systems. From here every boat, whether in the fastness of the North Sea, or even farther away in the Baltic, or in the middle Atlantic, was plotted and watched. The captains at sea were instructed to report in regularly, and every night the messages stacked up for them were sent from this operational system.

Most of Dönitz's waking hours were spent in or around the operations room, consulting with his staff, talking to incoming captains about their experiences, checking with engineers and gunnery officers about their problems. When the wicked weather of January kept skippers from reporting in, Dönitz grew depressed and worried about his boats. For Dönitz and his officers at this stage it was still a small and intimate war. He knew all his captains personally, and he knew most of the watch officers, engineers, and gunnery officers by name and by sight. At this stage of the war nearly all of them were his handpicked "boys" of the exclusive U-boat club. He knew many of the petty officers, too. He made it a practice, whenever he was not summoned away, to go down to the docks to see off or to welcome home any boat that was going or coming. Down he would come with the band and the pretty girls and the flowers, to greet the conquering heroes. The gangplank was laid across the moored U-boat, and the admiral stepped briskly aboard, walked straight up to the officers and crew lined up at attention, and greeted the captain with a hearty handshake. Then the debriefing began. So too came the staff members and the "blue mice," the young German women brought to France as confidential secretaries to the U-boat arm. Before all their eyes this winter the engineers of the Organisation Todt from Germany (who later built the shore defenses that caused Hitler to call the French coast *Festung Europa*—Fortress Europe—were planning and building the three enormous reinforced concrete U-boat bunkers, each capable of housing thirteen U-boats under at least twenty-five feet of steel and concrete.

Across the English Channel, the British watched this building with great interest, but no action was taken to interdict it. Perhaps at first the RAF did not understand what the Germans were really building, and Bomber Command did not have enough aircraft to meet all the commitments pushed on it by others. But the fact was that the British lost their chance to stop the construction of these bomb-proof shelters, and when they finally woke up to the problem it was too late.

This winter of 1941, however, the building was still in progress, and the facilities of the U-boat men were sparse. This did not prevent them from enjoying themselves ashore. The leave time in the French ports was one great party for the crews and the junior officers. Houses of prostitution were established and regulated, but this did not keep some of the men from going off on their own, and then showing up on the next cruise with a roaring case of venereal disease. That was one of the most unpleasant ailments of the U-boats, because of the close confinement of the men and the difficulties with the minimal plumbing aboard the boats. But it was inevitable, for the evenings were spent in drinking and carousing, and no one could blame these young men overmuch for their excesses. They were blowing off steam, and forgetting for a little while the enormous danger in which they lived every minute when afloat.

Some captains took more exception to their men's carousing than others. Otto Kretschmer was a strict disciplinarian. One night he looked out of his hotel window at Lorient and saw several of his petty officers, almost blind drunk, crawling beneath his window, hoping they could get past without his seeing them. Next day they were on report, and it was many weeks before they recovered the respect of their commanding officer. But the fact was that most of these hell-raisers were well-disciplined and cheerful sailors when afloat. A commander had to be able to forgive much, for the U-boat force was changing in every way.

In the old days, when young men like Kretschmer had trained, an officer was everything and an enlisted man nothing. A petty officer might give the command "Slope Arms" to his drill squad. If he saw a man doing it sloppily, he might single him out and order,

"Double quick march. Lie down. Stand up. Lie down. Stand up. Hop. Crawl. Run. Stand up," until the petty officer was tired of the game.

But in the new navy it was not that way.

The new petty officer would say, "Seaman Mayer, one step forward. You will now lie down."

It must all be done according to the drill book, and the seaman's feelings must not be hurt. In the old days an officer seeing a seaman's scarf improperly knotted at inspection might pull it all out. By 1941 he could no longer do that.

"Your scarf looks terrible. Untie it and knot it again" was all he could say. He could not touch the seaman.

The old guard called it a damned shame. The seamen called it liberation.

In the old navy, the lines had been drawn very strictly between officers, petty officers, and seamen. The discipline continued now, but the hierarchy was being broken down purposely. Lieutenant Schepke, for example, was the man who introduced the work squad to Lorient. He convinced Dönitz that when his men came in from patrol, all of them ought to be rewarded by shore leave and all at once. His solution to policing the boat, and getting all the repairs done, was to turn the U-boat over to an *Arbeitskommando,* or work squad, which would have a list of all that was wrong, and would clean and clear the boat so that when the real crew returned from leave, all was shipshape. That was a sort of democratization unknown before.

Also, in Lorient and elsewhere, the degree of familiarity between officers and men continued to grow. One reason was a shortage of space and facilities. In the old days a seaman would not dare come into an "officers' " café. But now an enlisted man was permitted to enter any restaurant, as long as he saluted (a Nazi salute) when he came in the door. If the place was full, he might even go up to a table where an officer was sitting, give the Nazi salute, and ask to sit down. What happened next was up to the officer.

Schepke had a lot to do with such changes. When he and his men were back in port, getting ready to go out again, he might suspend shore leave for a night and then hold a party on board, at which officers and men would get gloriously drunk and fall on each others' necks, and reach a degree of camaraderie that would have made Dönitz shudder had he seen it. But Schepke knew his crew. He provided them with English jazz records, which were just then the rage in Berlin, and all the schnapps they could drink on those special party nights.

For the captain of the incoming submarine at Lorient there was much to do. First there was dinner with the admiral and his staff, which was a gentle sort of debriefing at which the captain had to answer all sorts of questions. Then, there was the report on his patrol to perfect and submit. Dönitz went over every such report with enormous care. He was forever looking for evidence of changes in enemy procedures and weapons that would necessitate counterchanges by the U-boat force. The British Asdic, he had learned, was a very effective weapon, except that it would cut out when an explosion came near. Thus a British destroyer hunting a submarine would make Asdic contact, then make a run with depth charges, and the explosion of the charges would knock out the Asdic for several minutes. That pause in the search always gave the submarine commander a chance to change direction or depth and perhaps to escape unharmed.

After several days, during which Dönitz and his staff studied the U-boat's patrol report, the skipper would be called in for another session, this time to hear the critique of the staff. He had to answer for his use of torpedoes, for misses, for gunnery action or the lack of it, and for the speed with which he informed U-boat command of ship sightings and other changes at sea.

Many errors were made by many captains, and this was to be expected in a service where split-second decisions had to be made. Dönitz could be forgiving of all errors but one, and that was lack of aggressiveness on the part of a commander. A captain could do everything but run his boat aground, and still gain the approval of the admiral, if he was aggressive enough. The name of the game, as the staff knew full well, was to sink ships, and more ships.

With the increase in the number and size of British convoys, Britain's resources were stretched very thin that winter. The United States had given Britain fifty old coal-burning destroyers in exchange for naval bases in the Atlantic, which warned Dönitz in two ways. The old American destroyers would obviously become another threat to the U-boats on the convoy routes; and the increasing American presence in the Atlantic indicated an increasing American involvement in the war on the side of Britain. Yet, Dönitz's hands were tied. Hitler did not want to bring America into the war, and so, no matter what the Americans did, at this point they were immune from U-boat attack.

Dönitz was getting more oceangoing U-boats, but the British defenses were also increasing. Ninety trawlers had been delivered to the British Admiralty and went into service as anti–U-boat patrol craft. When the captains brought that information back to Dönitz, he declared war on trawlers, and after that no U-boat skipper was chastised for "wasting" a torpedo on a trawler, although it was indicated that if they could be sunk by deck gun it might be better. Also, that winter, the Flower-class corvettes ordered by Winston Churchill in 1939 were beginning to come into service. Every one of them was desperately needed, there was no surplus, and the increasing number of convoys were still underprotected. Dönitz knew it as well as anyone, and was determined to capitalize on Britain's difficulties.

After the first of the year 1941, Dönitz managed to get more co-operation from the German air forces than in the past. Until this point most of the help had come from the air arm of the German fleet. Now, with a slowing of the bombing of Britain, more of Göring's bombers were made available for scouting missions. The Focke-Wulff scout bomber was admirable for the purpose with its range and armament.

The improvement in convoy finding was immediate, and with the finding of the convoys, the wolf packs went into action more frequently. And the cooperation worked both ways. One January day a U-boat, trailing a Gibraltar-bound convoy, brought six Focke-Wulff bombers down on it, and the aircraft sank five ships. The results were ever more pleasant to Admiral Dönitz and ever more worrisome to Winston Churchill. Soon, Otto Kretschmer's total of ships sunk went above 200,000 tons. Other skippers were coming along behind him. The next month, Prime

Minister Churchill did Dönitz the honor of declaring the U-boat war to be the most vital part of Britain's struggle, and took personal charge of a special cabinet committee devoted to that struggle.

The spring months were very pleasant for the U-boat men. In March they sank 206,000 tons of shipping. One could no longer call it enemy shipping—or even Allied—because the Germans sank everything that moved in the blockade area, which included the entire North Atlantic outside the United States national waters.

Dönitz was getting his Atlantic-class 500-ton U-boats in greater numbers. He hoped to have 250 boats in this year 1941, or roughly five times the number with which he had started the war. The U-bootwaffe recruiting program was going full blast inside Germany. Dönitz could see already that the expansion was not an unmixed blessing. All too soon he would lose that personal contact with every boat. And it would not be much longer before the spirit of the U-boat corps would have to be maintained by other means than in the past. Also, with the Navy's increased attention to the U-boat corps came increased interest from the Nazis. The old captains and some of the new did their best to keep Nazis off their boats. There wasn't a one on Otto Kretschmer's *U-99*, for example. And despite attempts by the party to infiltrate with "political officers," Admiral Dönitz resisted on the grounds that there was not enough room aboard a U-boat for anyone not directly connected with operations.

The training program for officers had to be foreshortened, as did that for the crewmen. The war was only two years old, but already the U-boat arm had suffered heavily, and the rapid expansion had turned the old world topsy-turvy.

A basic change was the politicization of the force. At first, the U-boat captains were all picked men, and since Dönitz was not a Nazi, neither were his captains. But as the boats began to go down, and as the force increased, new captains had to be found, and it was not practical to bring them up over the four-to-six-year course from the bottom. So reserve officers, from destroyers and cruisers, and later from freighters and other sorts of ships, had to be commanded into the U-boat arm, then taught to manage U-boats. For many it was a great difficulty, for the U-boat was unlike any other sort of warship and the skipper was in charge to an unprecedented degree.

Often now an old reserve officer, with the discipline of the past behind him, would take on a crew of youngsters, perhaps half of them Nazis, who had never been to sea before. At the U-boat *Kommandantenschule,* some of the instructors were privately predicting disaster. The growing shortage—and Dönitz could see that it would become a problem, was of petty officers, the trained enlisted men who actually ran the boats under the supervision of the officers. Effort was already beginning to bring petty officers in from the surface fleet.

March was a hard month for Dönitz in another way. In ten days he lost four U-boats and three of his most highly respected captains: Prien, Kretschmer, and Schepke. Prien's *U-47* was the victim of a bulldog pursuit by a British destroyer. Kretschmer and Schepke were unlucky enough to be in the same tight convoy area which was patrolled by several escorts. Prien's boat went down with all hands; most of Kretschmer's crew were saved with their commander, as were most of Schepke's, except the captain. The British said Schepke was caught in the wreckage of the *U-100;* the Germans said he was shot to death cold-bloodedly by a British seaman when he went back to sink his boat after it had been disabled and deserted.

Kretschmer's *U-99* was caught by the destroyer *Walker,* and Kretschmer was taken prisoner, the most distinguished naval prisoner the British had captured in the war so far. The men of the *U-99* were carried to Britain, interrogated, and then established in a prison camp. From that camp, and later from one in Canada, Otto Kretschmer continued to carry on his war against the enemy. He and other officers managed to get in touch with Dönitz through coded letters sent to the relatives of the prisoners. Later they put together a radio sending-and-receiving set capable of transatlantic transmission, and finally they would attempt a mass escape from Canada that was narrowly frustrated, largely because of the excellent espionage work of British agents in Lorient.

But in the spring of 1941, suddenly three of the stars were gone. But more were coming up: Endrass, Hardegen, Lemp, Kuppisch, Kentrat, Rosenbaum.

In April 1941, the U-boats entered their prime. Late that month wolf packs took sixteen of twenty-two ships of the Convoy SC 26. They also sank 232,000 tons of shipping with the twenty U-boats on duty in the Atlantic that month.

The war's progress continued to see-saw: the British strengthened their defenses, the U-boats took a beating; the Germans strengthened the U-boat force and the number of aircraft helping it, the British took a beating; the British put more emphasis on North Atlantic convoys, Dönitz moved his U-boats to the South Atlantic, and sank more ships.

The British had one weapon in the war that they could not utilize completely for fear of compromising it; they had broken the Germans' most secret high-level codes, which sometimes referred to naval affairs. This spring of 1941, the British also perfected another device, High Frequency Direction Finding, or Huffduff. Soon the Americans were in the act, with a station outside Washington, which helped pinpoint the position of German U-boats for British naval authorities. But pinpointing and catching were two different matters, and at this point in the war most of Britain's antisubmarine effort had to be concentrated on simply guarding the convoys one by one and saving as many ships as possible from the wolf packs.

For a time that spring, Dönitz tried to integrate the Italian submarine fleet into the German Battle of the Atlantic. But it could not work. The temperaments of the two peoples were too different.

"These Italians are a loathsome race," said one U-boat officer to another. "They're so terribly soft, too. Even the officers."

The Germans were contemptuous of their Italian allies, far more so than they had any right to be. Ultimately the Italians took over South Atlantic operations, off Gibraltar and the West African coast. But the main Italian effort was always in the Mediterranean.

The war changed for the U-boat men in the summer of 1941, when Hitler attacked the Soviet Union. Immediately several boats were sent into the Baltic to wage war against Soviet shipping. But they found very little there. Other boats went into the Arctic, to interdict shipping between the British Isles and Russia. They also found very little. At this stage, the war against the U.S.S.R., which had to be prosecuted with submarines to please Hitler, was no more than a thorn in the side of Admiral Dönitz, who wished very dearly that the high command would leave him alone to sink merchantmen and thus bring Britain to her knees. Of all the leaders of the war, the one who understood Dönitz and his U-boats best was Winston Churchill, who saw precisely what the German admiral was trying to do, and exerted his major efforts to stop Dönitz.

By the summer of 1941 the little 250-ton U-boats were mostly retired or in the training program, and Dönitz had a number of the new Type IX, which were capable of making the voyage across the Atlantic and back with ease, or operating as far south as the Cape of Good Hope. The British answer was bigger and better convoys, and so Dönitz's U-boats concentrated on the South Atlantic that summer, where individual ships were far more frequent, and thus kept the sinkings up. The see-saw struggle continued.

In August 1941, the fears of the instructors at the *Kommandanten-schule* were suddenly realized in what the U-boat arm considered to be the worst scandal of its entire participation in the war. It came about almost as critics of the force might have predicted.

The U-boat was *U-570*, a new craft commanded by a new captain of the new school. His crew was a mixture of untrained officers, with a few old hands as petty officers and a very young group of ordinary seamen. Most of these men and officers had virtually no experience in submarines.

The summer war cruise of the *U-570* began with a grounding off Norway, which sent her back into the repair yards for two weeks. Then they went out again, destination Iceland. Off the coast, they were spotted by a British aircraft, which bombed and strafed, and Captain Rahmlow *surrendered* a U-boat that was completely unharmed and ready for action. So disgusting was this action to the Germans that when Rahmlow showed up at the prisoner of war camp where Otto Kretschmer was senior officer, Rahmlow was immediately put in "purgatory." No other officer would speak to him, except the two assigned by Kretschmer to deal with Rahmlow officially. For this captain had violated the U-boat man's code, laid down by Dönitz and incorporated into the tradition of the service: Under *no* conditions was a captain to allow a U-boat to fall into enemy hands. Rahmlow said he had surrendered because his U-boat was incapable of fighting. He gave up to save lives, he said. Members of his crew disputed his contentions about the condition of the U-boat and challenged his courage, but even if it were true that the boat was damaged (no signs were ever seen by the British of this), to Kretschmer and the others it was no excuse. Better that the captain and entire crew of one U-boat open the sea cocks and be drowned than that the U-boat be captured.

The Rahmlow affair, in fact, showed something new about the U-boat force. The Kretschmers and Priens and Schepkes were one breed. The demands of the war had forced Dönitz to lower the standards for entry into the U-boat officer corps, and Rahmlow was an example of what could happen.

Soon it was reported to the British that Rahmlow might be "executed" by order of a court of honor. Captain Rahmlow was hastily moved out, and ended up the war in a camp for airmen where his "crime" was unknown. It was the only occasion during the entire war when a U-boat commander violated the tradition of no surrender unless the boat was so badly damaged as to be unfightable. Even then the captain was supposed to make sure the boat was destroyed so as to offer no aid to the enemy.

What happened to the *U-570* was an indication of the importance of this policy. That U-boat was cleaned up by the British and turned into a British submarine with a British crew. Testing, they discovered all there was to know about this type of boat, and sometimes used the *U-570* to penetrate German waters. As far as the Germans were concerned, *U-570*—rechristened HMS *Graph*—was the most dangerous boat in the world.

The U-boat men came and went from Lorient and the other ports, stopping in the mess and the club to gossip about the war. The feeling among the captains that year was that the war ought to end in another six months or so. First, the Nazi armies would polish off the Russians; then General Rommel would reach Cairo and Alexandria, with help from the eastern armies which would turn back from the Caucasus. There was one problem; the accursed English submarines, which were doing quite a job of knocking out German and Italian shipping in the Mediterranean.

At Lorient, the submarine staff kept score for the U-boat men. By fall 1941, seven U-boat captains had their Knight's Cross of the Iron Cross with oak leaves, having each sunk the prerequisite 200,000 tons of shipping.

Dönitz was in constant conflict with the German high command about operations in the Mediterranean. He felt these could be best carried out by Italian boats and German aircraft, but as the war in the Mediterranean waxed and waned, Hitler's moods and demands changed. The sinking of the carrier *Ark Royal* and the British battleship *Barham* by submarines in the Mediterranean in 1940 had actually worked against Dönitz's arguments, and so he was constantly beset to keep a large U-boat presence inside Gibraltar. The U-boat men almost all considered the Mediterranean to be a dangerous trap in which anyone might be caught at any time.

Certainly for one U-boat, Lieutenant Schreiber's *U-95,* that prediction proved true. She was operating out of the Italian naval base at La Spezia, on patrol, when she encountered the Netherlands submarine *0-21,* which was serving with the Royal Navy forces. The *0-21* tracked the *U-95* and put a torpedo into her, and the men of the *U-95* crew who were not killed or drowned had to swim for it. Most of them were picked up by a British warship.

Most Americans did not know it, but by the middle of 1941 the United States Navy was deeply involved in the British war against the U-boats. Dönitz knew. On September 4, 1941, off Iceland, Lieutenant Fraatz reported that he had been depth-charged by a U.S. destroyer and that he had fired two torpedoes at the American vessel. It was the USS *Greer.* There was also an encounter with the U.S. battleship *Texas,* which was in the sights of a U-boat captain who did not fire. Then, on October 17, Lieutenant Schultze's *U-432* torpedoed the American destroyer *Kearny,* with considerable loss of life. The American commitment to Britain was certainly cemented. The war of the U-boat men was about to enter a new phase.

6-1 Grand Admiral Erich Raeder, commander in chief of the German navy, greets the crew of Lieutenant Otto Kretschmer's *U-99* at Lorient in the summer of 1940. After the defeat of France that spring, Lorient became the center of U-boat operations. Kretschmer, who had already made his reputation in the little 250-ton *U-23,* was given a brand-new boat, and proceeded to become the leading "ace" in sinking merchant ships. The crewmen are in summer uniform. Left to right: Kretschmer, Raeder, Second Watch Officer Horst Elfe (the short man) and Obersteuerman Peterson. Elfe later had his own boat, the *U-93,* which was sunk in January 1942, off Madeira. **6-2** This British photo originally appeared in a London magazine. So storied a skipper was Otto Kretschmer that after he was safely captured and in a prison camp, he became a sort of folk hero among the British, for he was their favorite sort of enemy: cool, polite, and very brave. His crewmen, too, were exceptional, and there was not a Nazi among them (see text). **6-3** The men who hunted down Otto Kretschmer. Left is Commander Donald McIntyre of the destroyer *Walker,* which sank the *U-99.* Right is Admiral Sir George Creasy, Britain's director of antisubmarine warfare.

6-1

6-2

6-3

Commander Donald Macintyre   Admiral Sir George Creasy

6-4

6-4 On the same day that Otto Kretschmer's *U-99* was destroyed, so was Joachim Schepke's *U-100* sunk. Schepke was not so lucky as Kretschmer: he went down with his ship. This poster had been put up around Germany months before, celebrating Schepke as Dr. Goebbels's U-Boat Man of the Day for sinking 18,063 tons of British shipping in the little *U-3* and then 104,380 tons in the *U-100* in the Atlantic. For this he had been honored with the Knight's Cross of the Iron Cross, and had he not gone down in April he would have been present to receive his oak leaves. 6-5 By the time a U-boat crew got back to port after two or three weeks at sea, the men looked more like pirates than spit-and-polish seamen. Here Captain Lehmann-Willenbrock is greeted by Generalleutnant Richter of the Wehrmacht at the end of *U-96*'s third war patrol. His officers and crew are to his left, lined up in order of seniority. Lehmann-Willenbrock later became a flotilla commander, and left the active patrol service.

6-5

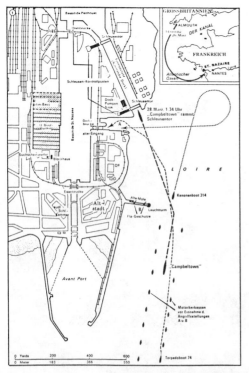

6-6

6-6 Here is the harbor at Saint-Nazaire, France, as the Germans refurbished it in 1940 and 1941 for their U-boat campaign. The impregnable U-boat bunkers are on the left side of the basin. The U-boat shapes show the usual means of ingress and egress—until March 28, 1942, when the British made a daring commando raid on Saint-Nazaire and the destroyer *Campbelltown* rammed the gate to the U-boat dock. The port was not put out of commission but repairs took several months. After 1940 Saint-Nazaire was the home port of *U-96*. **6-7** On watch. Bootsmaansmaat Witman (left) and Second Watch Officer Werner Hermann on the bridge of the *U-96* during the fourth war patrol. This patrol had begun at Saint-Nazaire, the first time that French port had been used by U-boats. It was extremely successful. As part of a wolf pack, on April 28, 1941, the *U-96* caught up with a British convoy and sank three ships, including two large tankers.

6-7

6-8

6-9

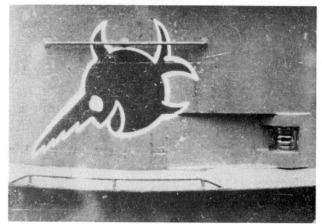

6-10

6-8 In the North Atlantic in the spring of 1941 this sight was all too common. Seaman Herting (left) and Obersteuermann Rademacher have their pictures taken aboard an ownerless British life raft. What happened to the ship's crew that abandoned their raft after hoisting the distress flag was another mystery of the sea. **6-9** Lieutenant Commander Heinrich Lehmann-Willenbrock of the *U-96* on return from the fourth war patrol in May 1941. The young lady is one of the many German actresses and entertainers who came to help celebrate the exploits of the heroic U-boat men. Skipper Lehmann-Willenbrock wears his Iron Cross around his neck for this official occasion. This photo appeared on the cover of the magazine *Erika*. **6-10** This idealized sawfish was the insignia of the *U-96*. When war began in 1939, the numbers of the U-boats were painted out but most U-boat men could recognize a boat by her battle insignia on the conning tower.

6-11 The distinguished career of Lieutenant Commander Lehmann-Willenbrock and his crew continued. Here Admiral Dönitz decorates two of the *U-96*'s seamen for heroism on December 8, 1941, as one of Dr. Goebbels's cameramen records the scene for the German newsreels.

6-12 Die blauen Mausen—the blue mice—were the German U-boat staff secretaries. They were called on to come down to greet the conquering heroes at Lorient when they returned from patrol. Captain Georg Schewe has just brought *U-105* into harbor after a most successful cruise, on which he had sunk several ships. He was also one of the first to use a new technique on this war patrol, taking on fourteen new torpedoes from the supply ship *Egerland* at sea. The officers in the black hats are members of the U-boat flotilla and command staff.

6-12

6-13

6-13 Danzig, winter of 1941. Left foreground is the *U-109,* one of Germany's newest Type IX submarines. The ships in the half-frozen harbor are naval support vessels, many of them serving the U-boat corps. **6-14** Captain Wilhelm Schulz (left) aboard the *U-124* with his first watch officer, Lieutenant Reinhard Hardegen. Both were to be leaders in the race to sink Allied ships. Like Lehmann-Willenbrock, Wilhelm Schulz was fortunate to become a staff man, and get out of operations before 1943. Hardegen went on to command *U-123,* one of the first to cruise off the American coast after December 7, 1941. **6-15** Captain Heinrich Bleichrodt of the *U-109* is congratulated by a general on his return from another successful patrol in August 1941. Bleichrodt was one of the most successful of the "wolf pack" captains in 1940 and 1941, working often with Schepke and Kretschmer. His *U-109* was a Type IX boat, a third larger than the Type VIIs and eminently suited for work on the western shore of the Atlantic.

6-14

6-15

6-16 The *U-124* that spring of 1941 went off to the South Seas to meet two German surface raiders. A clean-shaven Captain Schulz shoots off a flare to make contact with the scout aircraft of the German cruiser *Gniesenau*. **6-17** Teacher and student. *U-124* Obersteuermann Gerlach teaches Seaman Bayer the proper use of the sextant. As the war went on, more and more training was conducted aboard the U-boats on their cruises.

6-16

6-17

6-18

6-18 A *U-124* signalman makes contact with Schiff 41, the raider *Kormoran,* somewhere in the South Seas. **6-19** At left is the pocket battleship *Admiral Scheer.* At right, below the circular direction finder, is the raider *Kormoran,* Schiff 41, which enjoyed a successful but brief career in the South Seas. The view is from the deck of the *U-124.*

6-19

6-20

6-20 To the bow of the *U-124* come three waifs of the sea, survivors of the freighter *Umona,* sunk by the submarine on March 30, 1941.
6-21 Now a line is thrown, they take a tow, and will soon be aboard the submarine, not quite sure of what will happen next.

6-21

6-22

6-23

6-24

6-25

6-22 Just before the end. April 4, 1941: The steamer *Marlene*, in the periscope of the *U-124*. **6-23** From the deck of the *U-124*, a crewman photographs the steamer *Portadoc*, stern high in the air, as she heads for the bottom of the sea after being torpedoed on April 7, 1941. **6-24** Survivors of the steamer *Tweed*, sunk by the *U-124*, on April 8, 1941. There were too many of them to be taken aboard. They were given supplies, directions, and set back afloat. **6-25** Captain Schulz on the bridge, coming into harbor from *U-124*'s fourth successful war patrol, May 1, 1941. Note the pennants behind the skipper; each represents a ship sunk. So do the oil-soaked life rings hung around the conning tower.

6-26 By the summer of 1941, Saint-Nazaire was one of the U-boats' most useful harbors, for attacks on shipping in the Atlantic, north and south, and the Bay of Biscay. British ships heading for Gibraltar and the Mediterranean had to pass the Bay of Biscay, so the pickings were good. Here the *U-95* heads into Saint-Nazaire harbor behind the new *U-203*. The nomenclature is deliberately misleading. *U-95,* under Captain Schreiber, was a Type VII-C boat, built at about the same time as Kretschmer's *U-99. U-203* (Captain Kottmann) was also a Type VII-C boat. **6-27** Here is Lieutenant Heyda's *U-434* at Wilhelmshaven in the summer of 1941, loading supplies through the deck hatch. Behind the officer is the deck gun. Again, despite the high number, *U-434* was a Type VII-C boat, the most successful and common design for the Atlantic war. She did not last long; she was sunk by an aircraft off Cape Saint Vincent that same December.

6-26

6-27

6-28

6-28 The *U-43* sinks a trawler. Such a small vessel would ordinarily seem to be too insignificant for the expenditure of a torpedo, but in 1940 Winston Churchill enlisted a hundred trawlers in the service of the Royal Navy, and after that many more. The trawlers escorted convoys and patrolled coastal areas, carrying depth charges and deck guns, and Dönitz declared war on them.

6-29

6-30

6-31

RECREATION ROOM

6-29 U-boat prisoners of war arrive at the camp that will be their new home in England for the duration, under the watchful eyes of British soldiers, and the curious ones of a couple of girls, background. **6-30** Monteith Camp, near Lake Ontario. After the POWs of several camps in England had staged escape attempts for a few months, the British got tired of worrying about them, and shipped most of the U-boat prisoners to Canada. Of all the POWs the U-boat men gave the most trouble and were constantly trying to figure out methods of escape. **6-31** French washerwomen for the U-boat undershirts. Many of these women were happy to work for the Germans, but a number were members of the Resistance movement and used their daily activity to spy on the U-boat bases in France. **6-32** POWs at Camp Lethbridge, Ontario, Canada. The happy self-satisfied smiles are somewhat misleading. After Commander Otto Kretschmer was transferred to Canada, he set up an espionage ring that was the most effective the Germans had anywhere. He was in constant communication with Dönitz by radio and letter, and in 1944 organized an escape attempt that very nearly came off, foiled only by British spies at Lorient who learned that a U-boat was being sent to the Saint Lawrence River to rescue a number of U-boat captains.

6-33

6-33 A typical young German U-boat man, Seaman Paul Haberer of *U-31.* His U-boat was sunk in the Atlantic in the winter of 1940 by an aircraft. **6-34** The cemetery in Ontario, Canada, where some of the men of the *U-31* are buried.

6-34

6-35

6-36

6-35 Type VII-A. The scourge of Britain's
seas in those hard months of 1940 and
1941. **6-36** *U-48* was probably the most
famous of all the U-boats and had the most
successful captains of any. Here is Heinrich
Bleichrodt, one of Wilhelm Schulz's
successors.

6-37

6-38

6-37 Reinhard (Teddy) Suhren. A watch officer under Captain Bleichrodt, Suhren later had his own U-boat and became another of the prize-winning captains. **6-38** Clearing the ice from the deck of the *U-48* before she sets out on winter patrol. **6-39** The *U-46* with a conning tower banged up by collision.

6-39

6-40

6-40 Lieutenant Richard Zapp of the *U-66* at Lorient, on August 5, 1941. She was one of the most effective members of Dönitz's wolf packs. **6-41** Fending off. The *U-46* threatens to slap into the mole at Saint-Nazaire, as she comes in triumphantly in May 1941 (note brass band in rear). She is fended off by crewmen. Dönitz would not have liked that display of sloppy seamanship if he had seen it.

6-41

6-42 *U-66*, sailing from Saint-
Nazaire on another war patrol.
Everybody who can make it is on
deck to see the last of their liberty
port for another time around.

6-43 *U-68* sailed out into the South Seas to meet with the surface raider *Atlantis,* also called Schiff 16. They were discovered and attacked by British warships, the *Atlantis* was sunk, and the crew were rescued by submarines. This is the last photo of members of the two crews relaxing aboard the submarine, just before the trouble started. **6-44** Skipper Freidrich Guggenberger of the *U-81.* He is the daring captain who sank the British carrier *Ark Royal* in the Mediterranean in November 1941. **6-45** *U-81* in La Spezia, the Italian naval base, after the sinking of the *Ark Royal.*

6-44

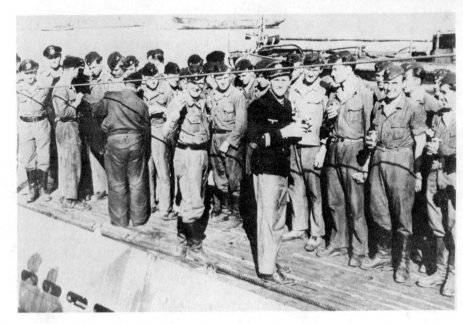

6-45

6-46 That wreck of smoke and steel is the mighty battleship *Barham,* pride of the British Mediterranean fleet, going down after being torpedoed by Lieutenant Freiherr von Tiesenhausen's *U-331* on November 21, 1941.

6-47 Lieutenant Freiherr von Tiesenhausen salutes the dock as he comes ashore from the *U-331* after his triumphal return to La Spezia, having sunk the battleship *Barham.* The rather tentative lady in the middle with the bouquet of flowers is obviously an Italian maiden laid on for the occasion. On right is Commander Öhrn, sent down to Rome to run Hitler's U-boats in the Mediterranean.

6-48

6-48 In the North Atlantic in the spring of 1941 things were not going so well for Dönitz. He lost Kretschmer, Schepke, and Prien in a very few days (see text). Then, on May 10, 1941, three British destroyers attacked Lieutenant Commander Lemp's *U-110,* and this was the result: the U-boat scuttled and the crew captured. **6-49** Some of the U-boat skippers were jolly pirates, some were martinets, and it was not hard to tell which were which. Here Captain Bruno Hausmann of the *U-127* goes ashore at Kiel, with full pomp and circumstance, saluted by his crew. Nobody is smiling.

6-49

6-50

6-50 On the other hand there were officers like Captain von Schlippenbach of the *U-453*. Here are some of his officers and the German movie star Christel Rienau at Pola, an Italian naval base. The top hat and uniform jacket decorated with pennants representing ships sunk were permitted on informal occasions for U-boat officers. **6-51** The *U-570*. This was Captain Rahmlow's boat, the only U-boat voluntarily surrendered to the Allies during World War II. The British, who captured it off Iceland, renamed it HMS *Graph*.

6-51

6-52

6-52 One of the first of the German U-boats to come into Lorient harbor. Note the crowds of Frenchmen on the quay behind.
6-53 The *U-65* in drydock in Brest harbor, September 1940. The capture of France revolutionized the U-boat war for Germany, making everything easier than it had been before.

6-53

6-54

6-54 The *U-65* leaving port at
Lorient in September 1940. In
these days, with no British or
American aircraft ready to pounce,
the departure of a U-boat was a
festive occasion and small boats
accompanied them out past the
channel buoys.

6-55 The *U-65* operating under water. These quartermasters in the control room respond to the orders from the bridge or conning tower. **6-56** A torpedoman adjusts the main tool of his trade aboard the *U-65*.

6-55

6-56

6-57 One of the new transatlantic Type IX boats goes to sea.

7. U-Boats Against America

December 7, 1941. It was evening in Berlin and Lorient when the radios crackled with the news that the Japanese had bombed Pearl Harbor. Had the Japanese been wiser, they would have given advance warning to their German allies, and Admiral Dönitz would have been able to make some preparations. But the truth was that the Japanese government never really considered its war with the West to be a joint venture with Germany. Neither Dönitz nor even Hitler had the slightest indication of the attack before it came.

Consequently Admiral Dönitz did not have a single U-boat in Western Atlantic waters.

In December, Dönitz and his staff assessed the situation. They knew very little about American naval preparedness in the Atlantic, except that the Americans had moved part of their fleet to the Atlantic several months earlier and now called that part "the Atlantic fleet." They could normally expect that a U-boat attack would initially meet with considerable success, if only because the Americans were new to the war, and their coastline, from Maine to Key West, was a very long one. "We believed that we should find conditions at least as favorable for the conduct of U-boat operations as those which had obtained a year or two earlier in British waters." But Dönitz also knew that the Americans were adaptable, and that with their powerful economy these favorable conditions would change. "It was, therefore, of primary importance to take full advantage of the favorable situation as quickly as possible and with all available forces, before the anticipated changes occurred."

What were the available forces?

As of December 8, 1941, the force of operational U-boats numbered ninety-one. Of these, twenty-three were assigned to the Mediterranean on absolute orders from Hitler. Three more boats were under orders to go to the Mediterranean. Six boats were stationed west of Gibraltar, to prey primarily on shipping bound to and from Gibraltar. Four U-boats were stationed along the Norwegian coast. That left fifty-five boats. Of these, thirty-three were in the dockyards in Germany and France, undergoing repairs. The repairs were dreadfully slow, because the demands of the surface fleet had created a serious shortage of marine labor.

Twenty-two boats were at sea. Eleven of them were moving either toward or away from their operational areas. Thus as of the beginning of America's involvement in the war Dönitz had eleven boats available to wage war against America, if he could use them.

He asked Admiral Raeder for permission to use a dozen boats, including six of the 750-ton Type IX-C boats that were stationed west of Gibraltar. These boats were too large for the shallow waters around the Mediterranean, because they were too easily located. Also, their basic asset, a large fuel capacity, was wasted in the Mediterranean area where it was not needed.

But Raeder was afraid to go against Hitler, who was urging every effort to bring the Africa war to an end so that he could throw more forces against the Soviets in the east. Dönitz's request was denied tersely. That left him only six suitable U-boats to send against the two-thousand-mile American coast.

On December 12 Germany declared war on the United States, and Dönitz was free to act. He sent his six boats out with sealed instructions: they were to move to the east coast of America. They were not to fire on any vessels of less than 10,000 tons on their way across.

Captain Hardegen's *U-123* was the first of the six U-boats to sink a ship. Hardegen broke—or at least bent—the orders. The ship was the steamer *Cyclops,* and she was only 9,000 tons. He sank her on January 12 outside New York.

Next came Lieutenant Commander Kals in *U-130.* He sank two steamers off the American coast on January 13. Hardegen then went on a virtual rampage, sinking tankers and steamers up and down the U.S. coast from New York to Cape Hatteras, until he ran out of torpedoes. His last kill was the tanker *Malay,* which he sank with his deck gun. The reports began to besiege the American naval authorities. U-boats had sunk: *Cyclops, Norness, Malay, Alexandra Hoegh, Olympic, Varanger,* and *Francis E. Powell.*

Then Lieutenant Bleichrodt showed up in *U-109*, and sank the *Halo* and three other ships.

Along came Lieutenant Zapp's *U-66* to sink the *Allan Jackson*, the *Lady Hawkins*, the *Norvana*, the *Empire Gem*, and the *Venore*.

The fifth U-boat to reach the American station was Lieutenant Folkers' *U-125*. He sank the *Olney* and the *West Ivis* in short order.

These first five U-boats then headed back to their French ports. Meanwhile, out in the middle of the Atlantic, a wolf pack of eight U-boats operating between Newfoundland and Nova Scotia sank nine ships.

When Hardegen's *U-123* docked, the skipper could hardly restrain himself. There was an enormous herd of victim ships to be sunk over there, he told the U-boat command. Every U-boat that went to the American shore was going to be successful. There was no question about it. For as Hardegen had discovered: the Americans had no antisubmarine defenses at all. Their aircraft were few and not suitable for antisubmarine work. The destroyers were held with the fleet. There were no convoys—Admiral King did not believe in convoys. If there would be convoys there were no escorts. The largest vessel available to the Eastern Sea Frontier, the naval command charged with coastal defense, was a 90-foot Coast Guard cutter. Most of the patrol vessels assigned to this command were not strong enough to launch depth charges and withstand the shocks.

So Admiral Dönitz was informed that his fondest hopes had been more than realized. A happy hunting ground lay across the Atlantic, where the enemy was truly defenseless. Immediately Dönitz dispatched Lieutenant Winter's *U-103*, Lieutenant Rasch's *U-106*, Lieutenant Gelhaus's *U-107*, Lieutenant Commander Scholtz's *U-108*, and Lieutenant Heyse's *U-128*.

They hurried across the Atlantic and found the same conditions. In short order they sank nineteen ships off the American coast. The beaches were actually blackened by the fuel oil spilled from the sunken tankers, and an oil industry council spokesman predicted grimly that if the sinkings were not controlled, Americans would be unable to heat their houses or drive their automobiles in the winter of 1942–43.

Prime Minister Winston Churchill had not expected the Americans to be prepared in the way that the British were in this third year of their war, but he had not realized how truly unprepared they were. On December 7, the highest ranking officer of the antisubmarine warfare section was a chief petty officer!

Churchill sent a number of British-manned trawlers to the Americans, to teach them antisubmarine warfare. He sent the chief of his antisubmarine warfare section to Washington, to give more lessons. He and they convinced the Americans that convoy was the only answer, but the Americans still had the problem of insufficient escorts. The Americans had already begun to learn, but it would take some time to produce the ships. The American answer was the "destroyer escort," a ship about the size of a corvette, much smaller than a destroyer, built for the specific purpose of escorting convoys and fighting submarines. But in the winter of 1942, the destroyer escort fleet did not exist. Neither did the escort carrier fleet that would come along later. The British had a few escort carriers on the Gibraltar and Atlantic runs, but not enough, and certainly none of them available to stop the slaughter on the East Coast of the United States.

So, Dönitz had launched another *Paukenschlag* (drum beat) and the U-boat captains were enjoying what they called a second "happy time" when it was easy to sink ships and there were not very many enemy warships about to give any trouble.

At this point, Dönitz's biggest difficulty came from Hitler. The Führer, it seemed, never would learn the necessities of the war against England, to concentrate the U-boat forces against her. Hitler was still demanding more power in the Mediterranean and now on February 15, 1942, he demanded concentration of U-boats in the northern waters against the convoys taking supplies from the United States and Britain to Soviet Russia. So Dönitz, with no increase in submarines, was given another "front."

With such difficulties, Dönitz's "boys" did remarkably well. In February, they sank 411,000 tons of shipping. A wolf pack consisting of the *U-155, U-558, U-162, U-158,* and *U-587* took nine ships from Convoy OSN 67 on one February night.

Then came March 1942. The U-boats sank eighty-four Allied merchant ships with a total tonnage of 446,000 tons. Churchill was alarmed. So were the Americans. They began to put forth more determined antisubmarine warfare efforts. Their convoys did some good, but the sinkings continued to be alarming in April. The real limiting factor on sinkings along the American coast that winter and spring was the shortage of Type IX-C U-boats. Dönitz was just learning that the Type VII-C boat could also be used for the long transatlantic voyage if the boat was converted with extra fuel capacity.

Dönitz did put every possible boat into the French ports, to operate against America. Bleichrodt and Forster and Winter made their second trips to the American coast. So did Hardegen. The Germans discovered the "soft underbelly" of the Caribbean and sent more U-boats to work that area and the western shore of the South Atlantic.

One of Dönitz's strongest qualities was his ability to sense changes in the pattern of enemy shipping and sea defenses. This March he saw something happening in the South Atlantic, and sent Lieutenant Commander Karl-Friedrich Merten in the *U-68* down toward Freetown. In short order, Merten sank the *Hexlenus,* the *Beluchistan,* the *Baron Newlands,* the *Allende* and the *Muncaster Castle.* He had gone out on February 11, and was back in port on April 13. It was a long cruise.

But the "long cruise" was that of Lieutenant Commander Lehmann-Willenbrock. He set out from Saint-Nazaire in the *U-96* on January 31, on the U-boat's eighth war patrol. He contended, against the best logic of the Dönitz staff, that a Type VII boat was perfectly adequate for the American station, and that it could stay on station long enough to be profitable in the matter of ship sinkings. On February 19 he torpedoed the *Empire Sal.* On February 20 he sank the *Lake Osweya.* On February 22 he sank the *Torungen.* That same day he sank the motor tanker *Kars.*

By this time Lehmann-Willenbrock was off Cape Cod. He headed for the Gulf of Maine and Boston. Suddenly he ran into a nor'easter, and a blizzard. Inside the U-boat the temperature fell to minus 5 degrees Celsius. On the bridge it was minus 15. It finally grew so cold he had to take the submarine down to let the crew warm up. He moved on. On March 9 the *U-96* sank the steamer *Tyr.* On March 23, the U-boat arrived back at Saint-Nazaire, Lieutenant Commander Lehmann-Willenbrock having proved his point. He had traveled eight thousand sea miles. That was Lehmann-Willenbrock's last cruise. Dönitz put him in command of the 9th U-Boat Flotilla.

What he had proved changed the war again. Dönitz no longer had to wait for more Type IX-C boats to come out of the German shipyards.

Lieutenant Erich Topp was the commander of *U-552,* another Type

VII U-boat, who headed for the American coast. Boat and captain were experienced: it was the eighth war patrol for the *U-552* and the fifteenth for Lieutenant Topp. The *U-552* was trying another experiment. One of the problems of the Type VII boats for the American station was that they did not carry enough torpedoes. But by loading four to six torpedoes on deck, the fighting capacity of the Type VII boats could be increased. The trouble was that in order to get the deck torpedoes below, the crew had to have a fine day and the U-boat had to surface and stay there for the reloading.

Topp soon shot off all his torpedoes, with very poor results. Then he began working over ships with the deck gun, and sank the collier *David A. Atwater* with ninety-three shots. He also sank another three vessels. On the night of April 8 the deck torpedoes were brought below. After that, Topp sank one more vessel with torpedoes, but when he returned to Saint-Nazaire, he was flying seven pennants—six of the ships had been sunk, against all Dönitz's advice, by the deck gun.

On Hardegen's second cruise to America, he proved that everything he had said about the easy picking was true. He sank eight ships in short order and went home.

Without doubt, the Type IX boats were showing their strength. Lieutenant Georg Lassen went out in the *U-160,* a Type IX, on March 1 from Wilhelmshaven. He moved up through the North Sea around Scotland and then west. On March 27 he sank the *Equipoise.* Two days later he sank the *City of New York.* On April 1 he sank the *Rio Blanco* and five days later the motor tanker *Bidwell.* Next, on April 9, was the steamer *Malchace.* Then, on April 11, the lookouts spotted an enormous ship and Lassen gave chase. She was so big that when he got into position he fired all four bow torpedo tubes at the ship and sank her. She was the steamer *Ulysses,* 14,000 tons, a really big one. The *U-160* went home with 43,000 tons of shipping to her credit on this one cruise. No wonder the total Allied loss for April was 394,000 tons—slightly less than the previous two months, but still a rate of sinking faster than the Allies could build ships.

The enormous U-boat success on the American station in the first months of 1942 excited the whole U-boat corps. There were forty superheroes among the captains now, men with their 100,000 tons of shipping that brought the Knight's Cross of the Iron Cross. There were nearly a dozen holders of the oak leaves, for their 200,000 tons. Almost any captain who came to the American coast could make his reputation, and with very little danger. There were still virtually no effective defenses. The first defense arrived on April 1—those British trawlers. But as they came, so did a new weapon forged by Admiral Dönitz: the "milk cow submarine."

As the young skippers had long said in their bull sessions in the bars of Wilhelmshaven and the cafés of Lorient, if only the U-boats had the range, what they could not do: stay out for months, move from one ocean to another, wreak havoc with the enemy's supply routes. Now, in April, out came the first of the tanker U-boats, the *U-459* under Lieutenant Commander von Wilamowitz-Möllendorf. They were called the Type XIV boat. Their purpose was to carry fuel and torpedoes across the Atlantic to the boats operating on the western shore. They could carry 700 tons of oil, meet with a Type VII-C, give her 90 tons, which was enough to carry her along and get her back to France, and then go on to fuel the next. One day in April, the *U-459* fueled her first Type VII, the *U-108,* off Bermuda. In the next few weeks she refueled fourteen other U-boats. Two other tankers were out in April, also fueling boats on the American shore and in the Caribbean. The effect was to just about double the patrol life and effectiveness of Dönitz's U-boats on the American station.

Here it was April 1942, the Americans had been in the war for more than four months, the U-boats had been cruising along their coast all winter, sinking shipping almost at will, and still not a single U-boat had been sunk on the American station. It had to be said that the German captains were becoming a little bit careless. And why not? Every captain who went back to Lorient or La Pallice or Saint-Nazaire and reported on the ease with which he had operated off the American coast added to this feeling of superiority over the Americans that the U-boat skippers felt. It was not like dealing with the British bulldog.

So more young skippers agitated to be sent to the American station to make their reputations. And as long as the practice was productive Admiral Dönitz could not but agree.

One such captain was Eberhard Greger, the skipper of the *U-85,* who had made three previous war patrols in European waters, without a great deal of success. Now Greger was heading out on his fourth war patrol, to American waters, to achieve great things. Greger reached his station, off the Chesapeake Bay, in the first week of April. On April 10 he saw how easy it was: he sank a steamer.

In the Atlantic, the U-boats worked in deep water, and when they first came to the American shore they stayed outside the 100-fathom curve for safety's sake. If someone got after them, having 600 feet of water to dive down into provided a certain sense of security. But in recent weeks, the Americans had grown cannier, and had moved their convoys into shallow water closer to shore. After a few days, when Captain Greger saw ships sailing inshore of him, and too far away to attack, he decided to move in closer to the shore, and soon found himself in very shallow water, 30 fathoms. A year earlier probably Lieutenant Greger would have hesitated before committing himself to such shallow water. But it was all so easy on the American coast, there were so few planes and so few escorts, and the enemy was so unaware, that the danger seemed light. So Lieutenant Greger opted to accept the danger, and in he went to the entrance to Chesapeake Bay, where the water was 164 feet deep, and waited in Wimble Shoals.

It was true that the Americans were a long way behind the British, but they were running to catch up on antisubmarine warfare techniques. One of the apt students was Lieutenant Commander H. W. Howe, the commander of the destroyer USS *Roper,* which had just been assigned to antisubmarine patrol off the Wimble Shoals area. As the British had learned a long time ago, the antisubmarine patrol concept was excellent on paper but not very effective on the water, because the ocean was wide and deep, and a patrol craft had little chance of happening on a submarine. With the convoy system, the submarines came to the convoy, and then the escorts went after them. But once in a while . . .

And this night of April 13, the *Roper* found the *U-85* on the surface, chased her, got into a turning-circle battle, got a hit on the submarine's conning tower with a 5-inch gun, and caused the U-boat to sink, leaving forty men struggling in the water. Then *Roper* depth-charged the area, which meant there would be no survivors among the forty. The Americans had just sunk their first U-boat, a little nervously, and rather messily, but they had finally done it.

The second U-boat sinking by the Americans did not come for almost a month. Back in Europe, in mid-April, the U-boat command was just beginning to worry seriously about Lieutenant Greger's failure to report in. But in the mess at Lorient and in the cafés, the U-boat officers were not worried in the slightest. They laughed at the puerility of the American defenses, and whenever a boat was assigned to go out to the American station, the captain was congratulated with many toasts and predictions as to the date that he would get his *Ritterkreuz*.

Lieutenant Helmut Rathke's chance came at last. The *U-352* was ordered to move to the American station and take a position just off Cape Hatteras. Ah, the golden hunting ground, where Topp and Hardegen had made their reputations! With joy and anticipation of great works, Rathke and his men hurried across the Atlantic to their station. But when they arrived they discovered that something had changed. Life off Cape Hatteras was not the way Hardegen had said it would be, with balmy days for sunning in the spring, and no enemy naval craft to watch for. On the first day, *U-352* had to dive to escape a snooping airplane. The same thing happened the next day, and two days later a patrol plane caught the *U-352* on the surface, and, as she went down, she was very badly rocked by two depth charges that dropped far too close to the boat.

After that, Lieutenant Rathke grew nervous. He wanted a ship and when a convoy that had been promised by Dönitz's radio failed to appear in the next day or so, he decided that he would attack whatever came along. He chose a small vessel, of coastal steamer size, and made an attack. He fired a torpedo, and was afflicted with the same problem that had nearly driven Topp to despair: no matter what they said back at Wilhelmshaven about the torpedoes being all fixed, this one misfired, exploded short on its run, and thoroughly alerted the crew of the U.S. Coast Guard cutter *Icarus*—for that was the vessel Lieutenant Rathke had so erroneously decided to attack. As it turned out, the men of the Coast Guard cutter knew their business, and they sank the submarine, and the survivors floated in the water—for although the Coast Guardsmen were good at sinking they did not know what to do about Germans floating in water. They called back to base, and after an hour or so were told to pick them up. Rescue them they did, and Lieutenant Rathke and his men went off to prison camp. They behaved admirably from a German point of view, revealing virtually no information about anything, which infuriated American naval intelligence (particularly because the British were so good at interrogation and learned so much). And Lieutenant Rathke did not get his *Ritterkreuz* at all. But at least he was not dead, as were so many of his compatriots. More were dying all the time.

While those battles waxed and waned some other strange adventures were being staged. One of the most poignant and indicative of the state of the U-boat arm at the time was the adventure of Lieutenant Peter Cremer in the *U-333*.

At the beginning of the war Cremer had been gunnery officer aboard a destroyer. He served there through the Norway campaign, and won the Iron Cross. In the spring of 1940, Dönitz was already feeling the pinch of the officer shortage and looking about the fleet for bright young men who would fit into his program. Cremer was an admirable candidate, and he impressed the whole U-boat staff when he was called in to see Dönitz one day in June. The admiral asked Cremer if he would like to join the U-boat corps and before the lieutenant knew it, he had said yes.

When Cremer began his schooling, he learned that the U-boat arm had already lost twenty-three boats, and that was why Dönitz was so concerned. The training program of the past had not allowed for real speed in producing officers. But now thirteen to twenty boats were supposed to be coming into service every month, and that put on the pressure for new captains and new crews.

Cremer had six months of training, including practice with the escape apparatus until he had mastered it and could make an "escape" from a sunken U-boat in a basin. His reward for his good service was to be appointed skipper of *U-152,* the last boat of the 250-ton series. In May 1941, Cremer's boat was ordered up to Norway and he patrolled out of Trondheim, without any particularly impressive exploits. Mine laying, convoy tracking, patrol, that was the way it went. But then in July 1941, Cremer was transferred to the command of the new *U-333*, even before she was built. He watched the building.

After launching and fitting out and trial cruises, Cremer and *U-333* were assigned to the Ziethen wolf pack, which was operating in the mid-Atlantic. Convoy chasing was the name of the game. Cremer's first encounter with a ship—a big tanker—was a notorious failure. He missed with six torpedoes, and the SS *Algonquin* went steaming majestically away (to survive the whole war, in fact). But after that bad beginning Cremer got the knack, and, on January 18, 1942, sank the *Caledonian*

Monarch, and then the *Vassilios A. Polemis* and the Norwegian *Ringstad.* That was the result of his first patrol. Almost. For on January 31, 1942, Captain Cremer spotted what was obviously a British ship (from her fittings). She was not flying a flag or showing any other identification.

He tracked her, torpedoed her, and sank her. Another glorious victory.

Then, within hours, triumph became tragedy. Young Captain Cremer had sunk the German blockade runner *Spreewald.* The men who had gone down in that rough, freezing water had been fellow Germans!

Cremer learned of it when his boat and all other available U-boats were ordered to stop everything and search for survivors of the blockade runner. Finally, *U-105* found three lifeboats, containing twenty-four German seamen and fifty-eight British prisoners of war.

It was a sad crew that tried to sneak into La Pallice after the forty-five-day patrol. No one came out to meet the *U-333* that day; there were no bands, no pretty girls, and no flowers. A staff officer from Dönitz's headquarters came down to the pier and sharply ordered Lieutenant Cremer to bring his logbook, radio log, and his dirty, unshaven self to the admiral's headquarters. The court-martial was awaiting him there. The charges were: disobedience in action, manslaughter, and damage to military property.

So the court convened. Cremer's defense counsel was Commander Hessler, who was Dönitz's operations officer and also his son-in-law. As the charges were laid out, it became apparent that Cremer had not in fact done what authority had thought. He had been in his proper assigned grid square. The *Spreewald* had been at fault, she had strayed from the course mapped out for her safety, and had thus managed to miss contact with *U-575,* which had been detailed to bring her into port. The *Spreewald* was the victim of the new sort of undersea warfare: fire first, and ask questions afterward. Since the Germans had adopted that form, the authorities certainly had no grounds for complaint when one of their captains did just what he had been taught to do.

One certainly had to say that Dönitz was fair. The verdict: acquittal on all charges. The *Spreewald,* said the court, had brought about her own destruction by failing to follow orders and report her position.

The whole affair was kept secret and the crew of the *U-333* was warned not to talk, for it would never do to let it be known that a German blockade runner, trying to make it safely home, had been sunk by a German U-boat. And so the secret remained until Cremer published his memoirs in 1984.

After this adventure, Cremer and *U-333* were chosen to make the long trip to America and back, although the submarine was a Type VII boat. He argued for the job, saying that his boat could easily make the 8,000-mile trip from La Pallice to Florida and return, and have the time to make good use of his seventeen torpedoes. Cremer explained his plans to Commander Herbert Schultze, who by this time had been made flotilla commander at Lohs Flotilla—another successful U-boat skipper saved from the deep by promotion to higher command.

The crew of *U-333* rigged up battens so they could fill parts of the drinking and washing water tanks with diesel oil. They would stack food in the toilets. The free bunks were filled with ammunition boxes and spare parts.

And when this was all done, Schultze (nicknamed *Vati* or "Dad") benignly informed them that theirs would be one of the boats with the services of a milk cow.

It was March 30 when the *U-333* sailed for America from La Pallice, a fine day on the broad Atlantic, with a long, rolling swell, and little wind. They stayed on the surface as much as possible, and much was possible in these days of the war, for they were south of the convoy routes across the Atlantic. The third day out they were surprised by a patrol plane, which bombed them, as they crash-dived. The damage was severe enough: fresh water plant knocked out and the repeater compass smashed. But they had been lucky; at this stage of the war the depth bombs used by the aircraft were not powerful enough to do the job of a real destroyer's depth charge.

So they moved along. Not far away was Freiherr von Tiesenhausen's *U-331*. Both boats were heading for the happy hunting ground off the Americas. They arrived on April 20, and met their milk cow, the *U-459*, and Lieutenant Commander Wilamowitz-Möllendorf filled up their boat with fuel, and with food and drink. The *U-459* carried a doctor, but at that point the men of the *U-333* had no use for medical services.

They began to hunt. First a tanker . . . but the tanker proved a formidable enemy: the captain rammed the U-boat, and very nearly sank her, and then he got clean away as the *U-333* went down below to nurse her wounds. They made the Florida coast, where they were depth-charged by patrol boats until Cremer thought the hull would burst. But after those experiences, they sank three freighters (while U-534 sank three and their other companion boat, *U-507,* sank six, and Bleichrodt's *U-109* sank three more off Cape Canaveral).

So Peter Cremer had a taste of the glory of the American station, but by the time he came back from that spring cruise and was ready to go out again, the bloom was off the rose. Considering what Hardegen had reported in the winter, the U-boat captains were astounded that the Americans had managed (with British help) to recover as quickly as they had. In the growing appearance of escorts and patrol planes lay the secret. There would never again be such a happy time for the U-boats.

Back at Lorient, even when Lieutenant Greger and Lieutenant Rathke were missed, no one knew what had happened to them. It was a long way from one side of the Atlantic to the other, and it was conceivable that they might have run afoul of a British plane, escort, or mine. No one really worried yet about the American defenses, and they did not worry for many weeks, even as those defenses were improved and air-sea work was coordinated. So Lieutenant Horst Degen set off in the *U-701* from Brest at the end of May on his third war patrol. Lucky Degen, he was going to the American station to make his military fortune. The *U-701* topped off with fuel at Lorient, and headed west with fourteen torpedoes. On June 16 the *U-701* attacked a big freighter, sailing alone, off Cape Hatteras. Degen fired two torpedoes—both missed—and then, wonder of wonders, he had to dive because an airplane came over his way.

A few days later Degen sank an American patrol boat. But then Degen had bad luck. Hardegen and the others had told these stories of ships sailing alone, making plenty of smoke, but Degen didn't see any of that. What he did see were tightly organized convoys, zigzagging back and forth, changing speed at difficult moments, and protected by too many escorts. That was not the way it ought to be. This was more like it had been around England.

On June 27 Degen worked his boat into position against a southbound convoy and fired two torpedoes at a freighter. Then he had to dive, for two escorts were coming straight at him. Several members of the crew heard one explosion but they could not prove anything because the destroyers gave the U-boat such a serious depth-charging that the electric motors were knocked out for an hour and several gauges smashed. These repairs were made easily enough but what happened to the freighter? Hardegen's tales did not seem true at all.

But on June 28 Degen had to take that back. He encountered a big tanker, the *William Rockefeller,* all alone, and torpedoed her. He was attacked by an airplane, which was rather different from anything Hardegen had reported, but at least Degen had a success. He radioed back to Lorient.

And then, he was quiet. Every day it seemed, the *U-701* was harried by American aircraft. It got so bad that he kept the boat on the bottom all day long, even if the air grew very foul. So it was on July 7. He had been sitting on the bottom for many hours, and finally late in the afternoon, when it seemed quiet, Degen tempted fate and came up to periscope depth. All seemed serene, so he surfaced, and zingo, out of the sky came a bomber from nowhere. It bombed, and the submarine began to take water and go down. Seventeen men got out of the boat, but they drifted fast in the current, and before the rescuers found them the number was down to seven. The rescue was spectacular, involving all sorts of sea craft and an airship, and Dönitz very quickly learned most of the circumstances. Just then, Hitler was again demanding that all boats be brought back to the Mediterranean. Dönitz sensed, with the great quality of his, that the bloom was off the American rose: this new enemy had learned how to fight back in the past six months, and it was time to move elsewhere. So the talk at Lorient and Brest and Saint-Nazaire about easy medals on the American coast ended suddenly, and the U-boat war took still a different turn.

7-1 If the escape lungs were to work in time of need, they had to be tested frequently. So one of the responsibilities of a U-boat skipper was to be sure that his "lungs" were run through an escape tank such as this one. **7-2** What the U-boat man of 1942 wore to come up from 60 fathoms and more and arrive alive.

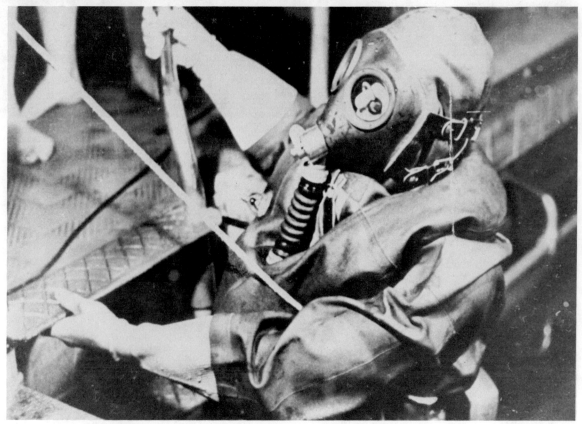

7-2

7-3

7-3 The *U-66* has just returned
from another successful patrol.
Skipper Zapp (left) looks on as
Commander Kuhnke congratulates
the men. By 1942 Kuhnke had
served his tour as a U-boat skipper
and was now commander of the
U-boat flotilla at Lorient.

7-4 This time it was one of the nurses who presented the flowers to Skipper Rolf Mützelberg of *U-203* when she came in from a successful patrol in July 1942. **7-5** The *U-203* has come up alongside a torpedoed and abandoned ship and the crew are preparing to go aboard to look for useful articles. Note man already in the water between submarine and ship.

7-4

7-5

7-6

7-7

7-6 From the gun deck of the *U-203* this was how it looked to take a merchant ship under fire.
7-7 The ship goes down. 7-8 The deck gun of the *U-203* from the bridge in heavy seas. Captain Mützelberg was transferred out and Skipper Kottmann replaced him. On April 23, 1943, the *U-203* was sunk in the Atlantic. 7-9 This time the ship torpedoed by the *U-203* is a tanker. The men in the boat will be given their position and perhaps a bit of food and liquor.

7-8

7-9

7-10 In the month of March 1942, the U-boats sank fifty-three ships in American waters. It was so disastrous a month for American shipping that insurance agencies stopped writing policies on cargo vessels. The U-boats concentrated on tankers, and that month sank twenty-seven. What happened when a torpedo hit is very well illustrated by this photo of the sinking of the tanker *Dixie Arrow* on March 26 by the *U-71*. Small wonder that the American beaches were black with oil. **7-11** But the U-boats did not have it all their own way. Here is a photo of the *U-71* being strafed by an American airplane on June 5, off the U.S. coast. The U-boat survived to get home, and went out many more times. She was still going at the time of the German surrender in May 1945, when she was scuttled in Wilhelmshaven harbor. **7-12** *U-87* (left) and *U-588* in Saint-Nazaire harbor, March 25, 1942. The *U-588* would be sunk by a Canadian destroyer two months later, while attacking a convoy.

7-12

7·13

7·14

7·13 One of the U-boats to go out early on the American station was Lieutenant Commander Lehmann-Willenbrock's *U-96.* Here he has just torpedoed the Norwegian freighter *Tyr,* and she is going down. **7·14** When *U-96* returned from her eighth war patrol on March 23, 1942, she put in at Lorient. Here come the crew out of the U-boat bunker. Lieutenant Commander Lehmann-Willenbrock is in front in white cap and scarf. These bunkers were absolutely bomb-proof, and withstood many attacks by bombers dropping the heaviest possible bombs. **7·15** Machinist's Mate Hermann Friedrich of the *U-96* at his starboard electric motor.

7·15

7-16

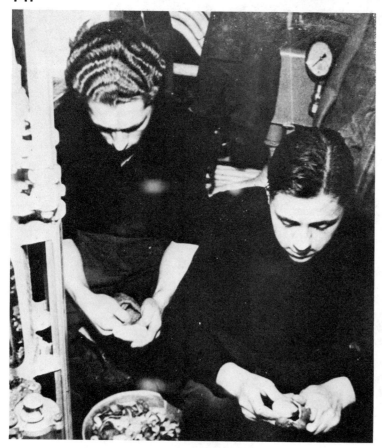

7-17

7-16 *U-103* under Lieutenant Winter was one of the second wave of U-boats sent by Dönitz to the American coast in the winter of 1942. Here, in mid-passage, members of the crew are clearing away wire that has fouled the boat.
7-17 Aship or ashore, it had to be. Here crewmen Schwambord and Gissel peel potatoes in the tiny *U-103* galley.

7-18 Crewmen of the *U-103* relaxing on the long voyage to America. **7-19** They called it the happy time, those months of winter and spring 1942 when the German U-boats came to America. They found virtually no defenses, and many a skipper, like Lieutenant Helmut Witte, made his reputation on such a patrol. Here his *U-159* moves into Lorient from its first American *"Feindfahrt."*

RITTERKREUZ ZUM EISERNEN KREUZ

Der Führer und Oberste Befehlshaber der Wehrmacht hat auf Vorschlag des Oberbefehlshabers der Kriegsmarine, Großadmiral Dr. h.c. Raeder, das Ritterkreuz zum Eisernen Kreuz verliehen an Kapitänleutnant

OTTO KRETSCHMER

Kapitänleutnant Kretschmer hat den englischen Zerstörer ›DARING‹ und 117 303 BRT. feindlichen Handelsschiffsraumes versenkt sowie Minenaufgaben mit Erfolg durchgeführt. Von der versenkten Handelsschifftonnage entfallen allein 27000 BRT. auf Unternehmungen, die ihn mit einem kleinen U-Boot unter den schwierigen Verhältnissen an die englische Ostküste führten.

Das Boot wurde im Jahre 1940 erbaut auf der

FRIED. KRUPP GERMANIAWERFT A.G. KIEL-GAARDEN

7-20 Citation for Otto Kretschmer for the Knight's Cross of the Iron Cross, awarded for his sinking of the British destroyer *Daring* in the early days of the war, an almost unbelievable feat for one of the little 250-ton "canoes" or Type II U-boats. **7-21** It was not often that an enlisted man won the coveted Knight's Cross of the Iron Cross. Stabsobersteuermann (Chief Petty Officer) Petersen was one of them. The fact that he served under the famed Otto Kretschmer didn't hurt. **7-22** *U-103* has just sunk a ship, and part of the crew is in this lifeboat. Captain Winter gave them instructions about their position and then moved away.

7-20

EIN VORBILDLICHER SOLDAT

Der Führer und Oberste Befehlshaber der Wehrmacht verlieh auf Vorschlag des Oberbefehlshabers der Kriegsmarine Großadmiral D R· h· c· Raeder / am 4. November 1940 das Ritterkreuz zum Eisernen Kreuz an Stabsobersteuermann

P E T E R S E N

STABSOBERSTEUERMANN PETERSEN HAT SEIT KRIEGSBEGINN ALS STEUERMANN AUF EINEM UNTERSEEBOOT / DAS UNTER FÜHRUNG VON KAPITÄNLEUTNANT KRETSCHMER STEHT / 12 FEINDFAHRTEN MITGEFAHREN · ALS WACHHABENDER OFFIZIER ZEIGTE ER AUF DER BRÜCKE GRÖSSTE VERANTWORTUNGSFREUDIGKEIT / ZUVERLÄSSIGKEIT UND EIN AUSGEZEICHNETES FACHLICHES KÖNNEN · BEI FERNFAHRTEN WAR ER MIT SEINER SICHEREN NAVIGATION UND MIT SEINEM UNERMÜDLICHEN STREBEN NACH ERFOLG DEM KOMMANDANTEN EINE WERTVOLLE HILFE · DURCH DIESE LEISTUNGEN ERWARB SICH PETERSEN EINEN PLATZ UNTER DEN ERSTEN UNSERER UNTERSEEBOOTSSTEUERLEUTE ·

WIR KRUPPIANER / DIE HAND IN HAND MIT DEN U-BOOTSFAHRERN AM BAU DES BOOTES ARBEITETEN / HABEN DIE MITTEILUNG VON DIESER AUSZEICHNUNG MIT BESONDERER FREUDE AUFGENOMMEN

7-21

7-22

7-23 Captain Hardegen (right) of *U-123* went to America to earn his fortune and sank six ships. The man on the left is First Watch Officer Selinger. **7-24** January 1942. Admiral Dönitz's *Paukenschlag* attack on America begins. Captain Hardegen looks from the bridge of *U-123* at a freighter he has just torpedoed off the American coast.

7-23

7-24

7-25

7-25 Captain Hardegen's *U-123* was one of the first U-boats sent to wage war on the United States. She sailed in December 1941. Here is the Christmas tree the men of *U-123* put up. **7-26** On the long voyage games helped pass the time aboard the *U-123*. Captain Hardegen is in the middle with Iron Cross.

7-26

7-27 Captain Hardegen on the bridge of the *U-123* with his watch officers. **7-28** Great success awaited Captain Hardegen and the *U-123* on their two patrols to American waters. Here they come in at Kiel in July after their second foray, pennants flying— and every pennant represents a ship sunk.

7-29

7-30

7-29 While the war in the Atlantic raged, other U-boats of the Type IX series began to move farther away. Lieutenant Jochen Mohr's *U-124* went into the South Atlantic and the Indian Ocean. Here she meets with the surface raider *Python*. **7-30** Lieutenant Mohr was at sea when he learned he had just been awarded the Knight's Cross of the Iron Cross. So there had to be a celebration. **7-31** Not all life on board a U-boat was grim. The crew of *U-129* indulge in a little horseplay on deck. *U-129* had several successful patrols, until August 19, 1944. Then her skipper, Lieutenant von Harpe, scuttled her in Lorient harbor to keep her from falling into the hands of the advancing Americans. **7-32** Through the periscope of the *U-129*, Lieutenant von Harpe watches the sinking of the ship he has just torpedoed in the Gulf of Mexico. The time was late June 1942.

7-33

7-33 The *Quebec City,* a freighter torpedoed in the Caribbean by the *U-156* during the summer of 1942. She has just been hit and the smoke has not yet cleared away from the primary explosion. 7-34 In the years of war Germany was very short of rubber. What better remedy than to strip victims of a few supplies? Here is *U-156,* a Type IX boat, on her way home from a war patrol in the Caribbean with trophies from a kill. Behind the stack of tires is the ship's insignia, the shield of the town of Plauen im Vogtland.

7-34

7-35 As the *U-159* steered into harbor on return from the war patrol, the crew hung out the American flag, taken from Lieutenant Witte's first American ship victim in this war.
7-36 This U-boat was *U-161,* the boat of the famous Captain Achilles, one of the men who sank 100,000 tons of merchant shipping in 1942. The Viking craft was her insignia. Here she has just returned from her third war patrol, safely, only to be rammed by a German patrol boat while entering the Lorient approach submerged. She made it into port all right, and made several more patrols before being sunk by an American flying boat off Bahia on September 27, 1943.

7-36

7-37

7-38

7-37 After Lieutenant Friedrich Guggenberger's *U-81* had sunk the British carrier *Ark Royal,* the boat was ordered by Hitler to come home for a celebration. Here the brass band plays to greet them as they come in at Kiel. **7-38** Lieutenant Guggenberger, who sank the *Ark Royal* in the Mediterranean, with Dr. Karl Frank, one of the leaders of the Third Reich, on a triumphal tour of Germany. Guggenberger was given a brand-new boat, awarded the Knight's Cross of the Iron Cross (*Ritterkreuz*), and lionized throughout the land. But the cheering stopped on July 19, 1943, when Guggenberger's *U-513* was sunk by an Allied aircraft. He joined Kretschmer and Jenisch and other captains as a prisoner of war.

8. Four Corners

In the summer of 1942 Admiral Dönitz was like a cat in a kitchen, faced with a mousehole on every wall. He moved his boats back into the middle of the North Atlantic and the Western Approaches, again attacking the convoy routes. He had several boats in the South Atlantic, looking for ships coming up the west coast of Africa and crossing over from South America. Because of the demands of Adolf Hitler, Dönitz had to cover the northern convoy routes to Russia and maintain a strong U-boat presence inside the Mediterranean. All this while he was being disappointed by the building program, to the point where his average operational force was not over seventy U-boats. And now Hitler ordered him to send twenty-six U-boats to operate out of Norway against the Arctic convoys.

The second half of the year opened with 101 U-boats available in the Atlantic, 59 of them at sea. But of those, with the comings and goings, only nineteen were in actual operations.

Then began what the Germans called "the fourth phase" of the struggle in the Atlantic. Once again, the emphasis was on the wolf-pack attack. On July 11, a boat of Wolf Pack Hecht found Convoy OS 33. *U-116* attacked, sank a steamer, and then the other four boats of the group moved in. Lieutenant Schnee in *U-201* sank four ships.

A week later, the six U-boats of Wolf Pack Wolf found Convoy OS 34 and shot it up. More and more. By the end of the month the Germans had again sunk ninety-three ships for a total of 454,000 tons.

In London, Winston Churchill's Anti-U-Boat Committee devised several new plans of attack on the problem. One was an increase in the number of small carriers ordered. The Royal Navy also began to put together hunter-killer teams of escorts, which worked with the bigger convoys. One of the most famous of these was that of Captain John Walker. And still another improvement (or threat, depending on how you looked at it) was the revitalization of the program of search and destroy from the air under Coastal Command, with the coming of more long-range bombers, specifically the American B-24s.

Mishaps began to dog the U-boats. On August 5 the *U-593* attacked Convoy SC 94, and sank one ship, then dived, under attack herself. *U-454,* from the same Steinbrinck wolf pack, also attacked, but was immediately forced under and depth-charged severely. *U-210* was rammed and sunk by the Canadian destroyer *Assiniboine.* All hands were lost. *U-704* and *U-660* suffered a series of torpedo failures. *U-176* and *U-379* sank three and two ships respectively, and then *U-176* sank another. *U-379* was sunk by the corvette *Dianthus,* and only five men of her crew were rescued by the enemy. *U-595* was damaged and headed home. *U-597* was badly damaged.

Certainly the U-boats were continuing to take ships out of the convoys, but the cost was growing higher every day. How the captains longed for those halcyon days, just months ago, when without concern they could sink any ship they could find on the American coast. They were still doing very well, on paper. August 1942 showed a figure of 517,000 tons sunk, but Dönitz was not fooled. Boats damaged, boats lost—there were far too many of these. And from reading the reports of the convoy battle in the Atlantic he could see that there would be more, for the British now were stepping into stride with the production and manning of escorts. The Allies were also developing new weapons, most valuable of which were new types of depth charge guns, capable of throwing missiles ahead of the attacking escort. The British called theirs the Hedgehog, and the lighter American system was called the Mousetrap. No longer did an escort have to get above the submarine to drop a depth charge effectively. These devices were particularly effective when an escort spotted a U-boat on the surface and gave chase. As the U-boat dived, the escort could fire its multiple missiles, and if it was close enough it had a very good chance of damaging the submarine. The new development in aircraft depth bombs also aided the Allies. The bigger, heavier bombs could do much more damage. In fact the combination of long-range patrol bombers and improved depth bombs would be the undoing of Dönitz's "milk cow" program, for the principal weakness of the Type

XIV U-boat was its slow response to emergency diving. Ultimately all of the milk cows would be sunk.

In 1942, the war also came to the far frozen north with a vengeance. On September 28, 1941, Convoy QP 1 sailed from the United States, to pass by Scapa Flow and make for Murmansk (1,400 miles) and Archangel (2,000 miles). Soon the convoy was joined by cruisers and destroyers. This became the pattern, delivering tanks and planes to the Soviets. By the winter of 1942, when the Americans were beset on their East Coast, the Arctic convoy battles were beginning. The first group of U-boats to set after them were members of Wolf Pack Ulan, *U-134, U-454,* and *U-584.* On January 2, the *U-134* sank the steamer *Waziristan.* The escorts got busy and the U-boats scattered. But on January 17 all three of the wolf pack attacked. Captain Hackländer's *U-454* torpedoed the British steamer *Harmatris,* and then fired a torpedo at a British destroyer. The U-boat then dived, but four hours later Captain Hackländer sank the destroyer *Matabele,* and not long afterward torpedoed an ammunition ship which blew up with gratifying fireworks.

The battle of the far north continued, in cruel seas and heavy ice. The *U-436* torpedoed a Russian ammunition ship, which exploded. But it was not all easy—none of it was easy in these waters. On March 24 the *U-655* was rammed and sunk in the Barents Sea by a British minesweeper, the *Sharpshooter.*

There were many acts of bravery and daring. Lieutenant Lohse in the *U-585* attacked the cruiser *Trinidad,* but unsuccessfully, and was sunk by the British destroyer *Fury.*

Back and forth. A three-boat wolf pack (*U-209, U-376,* and *U-435*) sank three freighters on March 30. The U-boats harried the PQ 14 and QP 10 convoys. Freighter after freighter went down. German destroyers, aided by *U-456,* sank the HMS *Edinburgh.* The Germans brought in air reinforcements, and by cooperation between the U-boats and the Luftwaffe sank five ships on May 25. The war widened. The big German warships *Tirpitz* and *Admiral Hipper* appeared in the northland, but so did British Admiral Tovey's task force, and battle was joined. As summer became fall the fight continued unabated. It was the struggle for the future of the Soviet Union, no less than that, over that chilly, often icebound lifeline of the convoy routes.

8-1 A staff officer of the Flotilla Weddigen (the 1st U-Boat Flotilla) notes that the *U-20* is in for a change of command and crew. The pins in the board note the situation of every boat in the flotilla, whether it is in operation, repair, or in harbor. The 1st Flotilla began operations at Kiel but in June 1940 moved to Brest where it remained until the Allies drove it out of France.
8-2 This photo shows the Trondheim (Norway) U-boat shelters under construction in 1942. The British missed their chance to destroy them at this time.

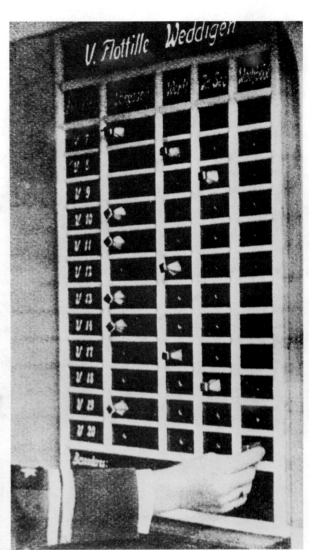

8-1

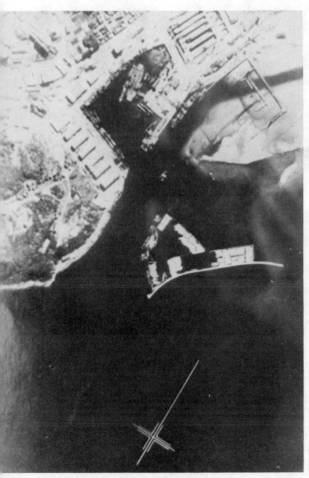

8-2

8-3

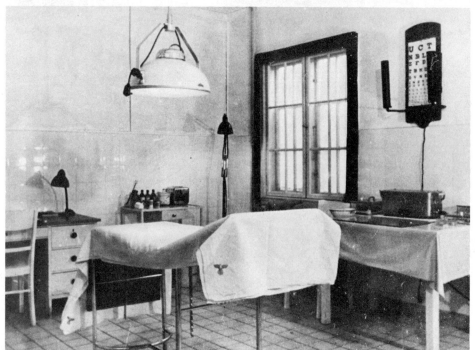

8-4

8-3 The steel trestlework is an indication of the strength of the U-boat bunkers built by the Todt Organization. **8-4** Operating room of the U-boat hospital at the 11th Flotilla base in Bergen, Norway. **8-5** The living quarters and headquarters of the 14th U-Boat Flotilla at Narvik. This was maintained until December 1944, when it was abandoned because of Allied bombing. **8-6** *U-48* again. Reinhard Suhren is on the bridge. He was First Watch Officer early in 1942. Later, as the skipper of *U-564,* he made six war patrols and sank thirty-three ships. He was awarded the *Ritterkreuz* with oak leaves and finally the coveted swords to the oak leaves, and then the diamonds. Moreover, he was lucky enough to go ashore and survive the war.

8-7 Admiral Dönitz aboard the *U-93* late in 1941. He does not seem very happy at the moment with Skipper Horst Elfe and his crew, as the looks on the men's faces indicate. **8-8** The *U-48* on her way home from battle. The object on the after deck is a buoy used as a plug for a hole created by a depth charge. **8-9** Skipper Horst Elfe of the *U-93* goes ashore from the HMS *Hesperus* at Gibraltar, to head for POW camp. **8-10** Here are the survivors of the *U-93* aboard the British destroyer *Hesperus,* which sank her on January 15, 1942, off Madeira.

8-11 Skipper Hans-Georg Fischer of the *U-109* does not seem to like what he sees off to his right. He moved up to take command of the 2nd U-Boat Flotilla. Skipper Heinrich Bleichrodt took over the *U-109*.
8-12 It was the same with every navy in the world. When a ship crossed the equator, old Father Neptune emerged from the depths to initiate into the Kingdom of the Sea all those "pollywogs" who had never crossed the line before. Here Neptune and his retainers hold court aboard the *U-105*. The blessings of the old king did not help *U-105* much, she was sunk off Dakar a few months later.

8-12

8-11

8-13 Here Captain Bleichrodt's *U-109* has stopped a fishing boat to trade rum and tobacco for fresh fish. Bleichrodt later went on to command the 22nd U-Boat Flotilla and the *U-109* was given to Lieutenant Schramm. She was sunk in May 1943 in the Bay of Biscay. **8-14** *U-116* meets *U-406,* one of Dönitz's milk cow submarines, to take on fuel and food and torpedoes on the American station.

8-15

8-15 *U-117,* shown here, was a Type X-B U-boat, a minelayer. The gratings in foreground are stowage compartments for the mines. The crew loads one mine. **8-16** The after end of the minelayer *U-217,* showing aft mine stowage. She is tied up alongside the battleship *Deutschland* in Danzig harbor.

8-16

8-17

8-17 Another submarine is launched to join Dönitz's fleet. This one is the *U-119*. She was sunk in June 1943, off the Spanish coast.

8-18

8-18 For some captains, champagne was brought out when their U-boat sank a ship. Aboard the *U-130* that was the custom. Skipper Kals (left) has a glass, while First Watch Officer Helmut Ellmenreich stands by to pour again. **8-19** The *U-130* had a very successful cruise that summer of 1942 on the American station. She sank the *Danmark,* above, on July 30 . . .

8-19

8-20 . . . and the tanker *Nalmange* a few
days later. **8-21** One of the boats from
the *Nalmange* comes alongside the
U-130, the men drenched in oil. **8-22**
On board they get a meal and some
drinks, but what then? The U-boat cannot
carry them all the way back to Germany.
So they get back into their boat and
are told how to make it to shore.

8-22

8-23

8-23 Sometimes, to a man of the sea, the sinking of a ship would be particularly painful. Here is the 30-ton sailing ship *Nueva Alta Gracia,* which the *U-161* sank by gunfire on June 16, 1942. The skipper of the *U-161* was Lieutenant Achilles, who ran up quite a record for himself before the *U-161* was sunk by a flying boat off Bahia about a year later.

8-24 Some U-boats seemed to generate seamen. *U-93* was certainly one of these. One of her best petty officers, Klaus Schaele, is here on the bridge of the submarine in Kiel harbor. **8-25** Lieutenant E. Hoffmann and his watch officers crowd the bridge as the *U-451* leaves Lorient on the start of another war cruise. Note flowers from the well-wishers at the right. But the flowers did not help. The *U-451* headed for the Mediterranean and was sunk off Gibraltar by an aircraft four days before Christmas 1941.

8-24

8-25

8-27

8-28

8-26 A distinguished crew from the *U-93*. Left, Lieutenant Clausen, Lieutenant von Tiesenhausen, Skipper Korth, and Lieutenant Gretschel. Clausen later had the *U-182*, which was sunk in the South Atlantic with all hands. Von Tiesenhausen was skipper of the *U-331*, which sank the *Barham* and later was captured (and scuttled) off North Africa. Korth went ashore to survive the war. Gretschel became skipper of the *U-707* and went down with her when she was sunk by a British aircraft in the Bay of Biscay.

8-27 Lieutenant Kuppisch's *U-94* (left) and Korth's *U-93* at Saint-Nazaire in 1942. Kuppisch won the *Ritterkreuz* for his feats, and took over the *U-847*. She was sunk in the South Atlantic by aircraft from the U.S. escort carrier *Card* on August 27, 1943. The skipper and all hands were killed.

8-28 Repairing the rudder of the *U-127*. Someone always had to go overboard. This time it was Radioman Eangle. The *U-127* did not last much longer. The *U-127* went down to an escort off Gibraltar two weeks before Christmas 1941. All hands were lost.

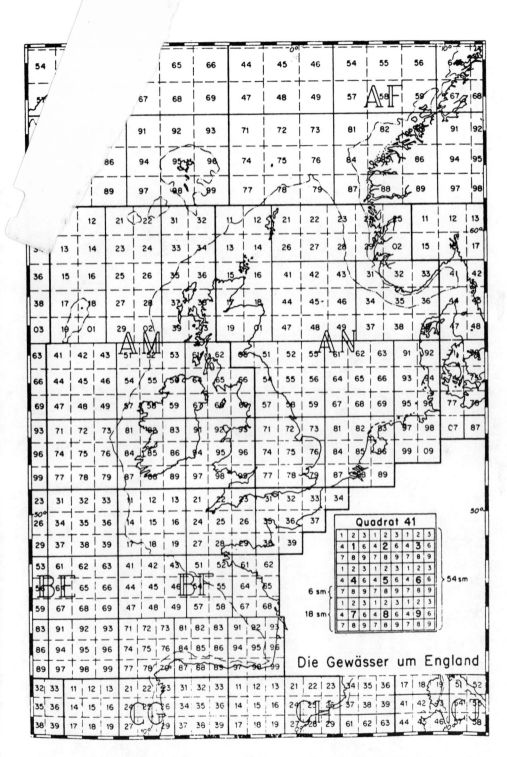

Quadrat 41

Die Gewässer um England

Squared chart of British waters used by U-boat captains for grid references.

9. "The Med"

Adolf Hitler never understood the truth in Admiral Dönitz's statement before the war that if the German navy would give him 300 submarines, he would give them victory over England.

Even after war had begun, and it was apparent from Winston Churchill's activities that one of his major concerns was the U-boat war, Hitler did not recognize the absolute importance for Germany to pursue the war against commerce and thus starve out the British. No, the Austrian corporal was an army man through and through, and he thought of his war as a land war with appurtenances. Thus, the U-boats were always considered by Hitler to be just another arm of the integrated services under his supreme command as strategist. There is no more striking illustration of this blind spot than in Hitler's use of the U-boat arm in the Mediterranean.

The war began in Northern Europe, but soon enough spread south. Greece was overrun. The Germans and Italians began their push to take all of North Africa. After France fell it seemed likely that they would succeed.

The war in North Africa was a land war, fought with tanks, infantry, and aircraft. The naval power came into play to keep the supply lines open. Britain was very effective with her submarines and surface craft as the land battle ebbed and flowed. The Germans were particularly effective in the air, with their bombers and fighters supporting the troops and attacking the British supply ships. But the German U-boat force was never comfortable in the Mediterranean, as noted, although U-boats enjoyed some remarkable successes there from 1940 on, including the sinking of the carrier *Ark Royal* and the battleship *Barham*.

U-boats were in the North Atlantic, South Atlantic, Arctic—and then Hitler insisted on *more* for the Mediterranean to try to push the Afrika Korps to victory. In September 1941 the first six Atlantic U-boats crossed through the Straits of Gibraltar beneath the noses of the British. It sounded very brave—but as Dönitz and his staff knew, the Mediterranean could very well be the deep-water coffin for the U-boat corps.

But now they all had to put a brave face on it. The 23rd U-Boat Flotilla was headquartered in Salamis. Other ports for the U-boat men were the Italian bases of La Spezia and Pola, where the 29th Flotilla set up in October 1941.

U-boat operations were controlled from Rome, whence Commander Öhrn had now come (another successful skipper saved) to be commander of U-boats in the Mediterranean. He would operate from the Italian navy ministry, with his radio transmitters in the Campagna, seven miles from Rome.

The plan was to bring twenty-six boats into the Mediterranean. Dönitz begrudged Hitler every one of them; he knew they should be out on the Atlantic cutting Britain's lifeline, not cooped up in this shallow sea where they were in constant danger.

In they came: Guggenberger in *U-81*, von Tiesenhausen in *U-331*, and others in *U-75, U-97, U-79, U-205*. Guggenberger sank the British carrier *Ark Royal* one October day, right in the middle of a convoy of battleships and destroyers.

On November 15, 1941, the four boats of the Gruppe Arnauld gathered at La Spezia. Along came *U-433*, under Lieutenant Ey, to be sunk ignominiously by the corvette *Marigold,* a reminder of shallow-water dangers. Poor Ey, his was the first boat lost in the Med.

Late in November the pack was out, moving around Ras Gibeisa and Tobruk. The orders now were to somehow further the German defense, for the British had launched a great offensive. And on November 25, von Tiesenhausen sank the British battleship *Barham* with three torpedoes. What a feat! It put him then and there into that select group of captains of the *Ritterkreuz.*

But aside from such heroic exploits, the presence of the German U-boats in the Mediterranean was not a success. The *U-95* was sunk by the Dutch submarine *O-21*, betrayed by phosphorescence and a little carelessness at night. *U-96* and *U-558* were badly damaged by British bombers. By the end of November, Dönitz had to count seventeen of his U-boats in the Mediterranean and the waters just outside it, and he did not like the results he was getting. He did not want to put any more in there. But Hitler was most insistent, and the boats had to be sent down to please the Führer. So they kept coming. Their greatest danger came from the hawkeyed army of British aircraft in the area. The patrols were constant, the water shallow, and the danger continued to be great. *U-432* was bombed and had to go home for repairs. *U-208* was sunk by the British corvette *Bluebell*. *U-206* was caught on the surface by a bomber and sunk on the last day of November. And so it went, a necessary service—the Führer said it was necessary—but a most unsatisfactory duty for the U-boat men.

In January 1942 there were twenty-one U-boats in the Mediterranean. Their task: to attack along the African and Syrian coasts, from Suez to Tobruk. But the proof that the sort of warfare being waged in the Mediterranean was better left to the Italians was not long in coming. On January 9, Lieutenant Schauenburg's *U-577* was sunk by an aircraft. Schauenburg, one of the aces of the Atlantic, was another sacrifice to Hitler's blindness. Three days later Lieutenant Fischel's *U-374* was sunk with a torpedo from the British submarine *Unbeaten*. So January began disastrously for the U-boat corps in the Mediterranean. To be sure, *U-77* sank the British destroyer *Kimberley* off Tobruk, and *U-133* sank the destroyer *Gurkha*, but this sort of warship trade-off was a misuse of the U-boats, as Dönitz knew. The British had more corvettes and destroyers than Dönitz had U-boats. And they were building them faster.

Yet that was how it went: in March the crew of *U-133*, still glorying in the victory over the *Gurkha*, were lost to the war when the U-boat hit a mine near Salamis. Lieutenant Fraatz's *U-652* sank two destroyers and a naval tanker. All very well, but such action was not winning the battle of the Mediterranean for Hitler. The pickings were slim, so slim that Skipper Guggenberger in *U-81* was happy to find a sailing craft off the Palestinian coast and sink her. But more typical of the U-boat situation was the story of the *U-74*, which in the spring of 1942 was under the command of Lieutenant Friedrich Ende. The boat set out from La Spezia on the first patrol under this new captain. On May 2 the U-boat was in the middle of the western Mediterranean when along came several planes from British Squadron 202. They dived, strafed, and forced the boat underwater. They radioed for assistance; up came the destroyers *Wishart* and *Wrestler*, and soon the *U-74* went to the bottom, victim of combined air-sea search and the new, improved British depth charges.

Back and forth it continued:

The *U-77* sank the destroyer escort *Grove* and the *U-205* sank the cruiser *Hermione*. But the *U-568* went down to three destroyers, and *U-652* was bombed so severely that she was a total wreck and her crew had to be rescued by the *U-81,* which then sank the *U-652.*

The U-boat war in the Mediterranean was far more a "military" fight than anywhere else in the struggle between Germany and the Allied powers. The Italians were as effective if not more so than the Germans in sinking Allied merchant shipping.

For the U-boats, the problem was that they had been placed in the wrong place at the wrong time. In the first six months of 1942, U-boats and Italian submarines sank 585 ships, by far the most of them in American waters, and in some months the sinking passed 400,000 tons. But a new factor had entered the picture: the enormous American production capacity. In that summer of 1941, anticipating the future, Dönitz's staff saw with horror that they would have to sink 700,000 tons of ships a month to keep up with the Allied shipbuilding programs, and they were not doing it. Nor could they do it, if Hitler continued to insist that the U-boat force be moved hither and thither to respond to every tactical change in the land war.

In a sense the most visible successes of the U-boat corps in the Mediterranean played against Admiral Dönitz, as on August 10, 1942. The British had a mighty convoy at sea, bringing materials for General Montgomery's drive against the Afrika Korps. When it was discovered, Lieutenant Rosenbaum's *U-73* was sent from La Spezia to attack and, on the morning of August 11, Rosenbaum found a large element of the British fleet, including three aircraft carriers, two battleships, seven cruisers, and twenty-five destroyers, guarding fifteen merchant ships. Rosenbaum caught sight of the carrier HMS *Eagle* and moved in to attack. He fired four torpedoes, they all hit, and the *Eagle* went to the bottom with two hundred and sixty men of her crew.

When Rosenbaum brought the *U-73* back to La Spezia, a representative came from the Rome submarine command to greet him. Flowers on the dock. A band. Pretty girls. It was all there and a senior officer in gold braid, Captain Kreisch, to make a little speech while he handed out medals.

"The sinking of the *Eagle* is a masterpiece of proper tactics and an unusually courageous U-boat attack. As soon as Rosenbaum recognized the carrier, he placed all on one card, and he played it."

It was not long afterward, however, that *U-73* was attacked at sea, damaged so severely that she sprang an apparently irreparable oil leak, and had to be sent home for major repairs. For such successes as the sinking of the *Eagle,* the U-boat corps was still paying a high price.

One of the great intelligence successes of the war, managed by the British, was the concealment from the Germans of the invasion of North Africa in November 1942. German intelligence failed completely to pick up the scent. On November 4, the naval high command ordered Dönitz to replace four U-boats sunk in the Med in recent weeks. That was all. No mammoth force was assembled to close up Gibraltar—as it might have been. And when the invaders came, the Axis powers were completely surprised. Consequently, Admiral Dönitz's U-boats played virtually no part in the attempts to stop the invasion in the early days.

On November 8, at 6:30 in the morning, Dönitz had a call from Berlin. The Americans had landed on the Moroccan coast, said Admiral Raeder's staff officer. Dönitz immediately began drafting orders: all boats between the Bay of Biscay and the Cape Verde Islands would move to the Moroccan coast. A few hours later operations in the North Atlantic were canceled and those boats, too, were sent to the Mediterranean, or to the Atlantic waters west of Gibraltar.

But when the U-boats got to the Med, they found something new: enormously powerful British and American air and naval forces guarding the convoys and the supply lines. As Dönitz put it, "they were so strongly protected by escort vessels and aircraft that the U-boats could find no loophole for an attack."

The U-boats had to remain almost continuously submerged, finding it difficult to come up even to charge their batteries, which took several hours. In the next few days two boats were lost and four others damaged so badly that they had to go to base for repairs.

Dönitz knew that his boats were being wasted here in an impossible attempt to stem a tide. He protested. The high command ignored him. On November 16 Raeder ordered Dönitz to replace all the sunk and damaged boats in the Mediterranean, and to bring down more boats from the North Atlantic so that at all times twenty U-boats would be working off Gibraltar and Morocco.

Dönitz objected again.

Again he was unsuccessful, except that he did persuade the high command to cut the number of boats from twenty to twelve.

The boats came down. They accomplished nothing, they found no convoys, they sank no ships. Finally, the naval high command realized that Dönitz knew whereof he spoke, and, just before Christmas 1942, allowed him to move his boats as he wished. Germany's U-boat operations against the Allied North African invasion came to a sudden end, and Dönitz went back to sinking ships in the Bay of Biscay and in the Atlantic.

Still, in December 1942, in accordance with Hitler's demands, those four new U-boats were already moving into the Mediterranean. *U-573, U-75,* and *U-559* came in, along with *U-568.* At the end of the month Dönitz responded to demands of higher authority by upgrading the Italian U-boat command. Captain Leo Kreisch was sent down to Rome to take over from Commander Öhrn.

9-1

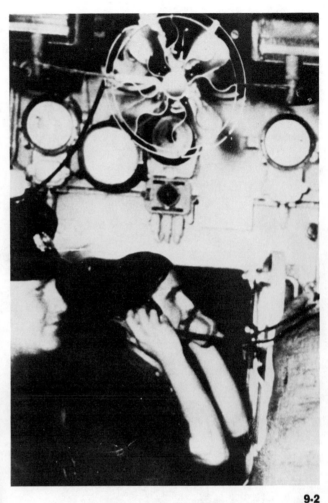

9-3

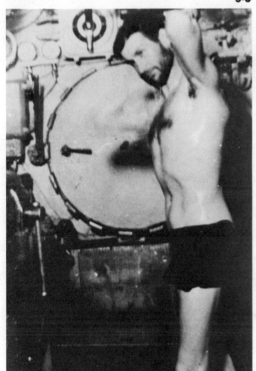

9-2

9-1 At sea, when it breaks, somebody has to fix it. The *U-67*'s deck gun broke down in mid-Atlantic on December 13, 1941. Lieutenant Karl-Heinz Wiebe was the gunnery officer and so had to go out on the sea-drenched deck to repair the gun . . . **9-2** . . . while the bridge talker told them down in the engine room what to do to keep the boat a little more stable for the lieutenant and his crew on deck. **9-3** In winter in the Atlantic, the best place for a bath was the nice, warm diesel room. The *U-67*'s Lieutenant Beutzt takes advantage of it.

9-4

9-5

9-7

9-4 The *U-67* comes into Kiel harbor before she surfaces. **9-5** Having finished his inspection of *U-67*, Flotilla Commander Victor Schütze returns to the dock. **9-6** The *U-67* meets another Type VII boat off Gibraltar and the signalman takes over. **9-7** *U-67* in the Kiel Canal.

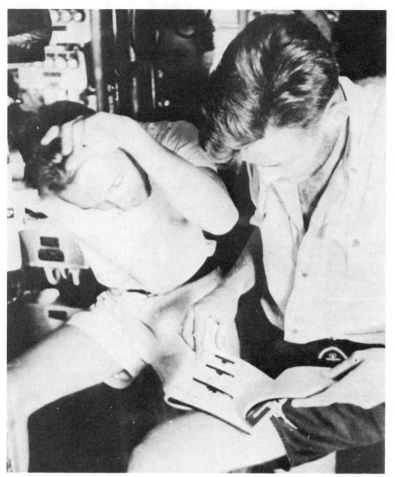

9-8 Skipper Rosenbaum of the *U-73* has seen a carrier through the periscope. He hangs onto the periscope and watches as First Watch Officer Deckert thumbs through the warship identification book. **9-9** It is HMS *Eagle.* Captain Rosenbaum's *U-73* has just torpedoed the carrier HMS *Eagle* in the Mediterranean, and she will soon sink. The photo is taken through the periscope.

9-9

9-10 And when the *U-73* returned to La Spezia, up went the very special pennant to show what they had done. Later Skipper Rosenbaum went to a shore job, and First Officer Deckert took over the *U-73*. He had some successes, but in December 1943 the *U-73* was sunk by two American destroyers off Oran. **9-11** Once the *Eagle* sank, the torpedo gang lost no time in claiming the victory.

9-12

9-13

9-14

9-12 Lieutenant Udo Heilmann, the skipper of *U-97.* He later took over *U-389,* which was sunk with all hands by a British aircraft in October 1943. **9-13** Officers and petty officers of the *U-97* at La Spezia. Flotilla chief Captain Becker congratulates Skipper Heilmann on victories. Between them, in the dashing overcoat, is an Italian submarine officer. **9-14** Admiral Dönitz and his staff at Lorient await the arrival of one of their U-boats from a successful patrol.

10. The Atlantic War, Phase 3

With the release of his U-boats from involuntary operations in the Mediterranean at Christmas time 1942, Admiral Dönitz was in a position to renew his assaults on the British Atlantic convoys.

Actually, the sinkings in October (619,000 tons) and November (729,000 tons) seemed to show an excellent record. But Dönitz knew that the reason was that the Allies had been forced to strip much of the power from their convoy escort groups in order to mount the invasion in North Africa. In December, when the U-boats moved to the Mediterranean by order of Hitler, the sinkings fell to 330,000 tons.

But looking back on 1942, Dönitz could permit himself some self-congratulations. The U-boats had sunk 1,160 Allied ships that year—a total of 6,000,000 tons. So far, the U-boat losses had not been serious enough to worry Dönitz very much. The percentage had never gone above 10 percent per year, and in 1942 was less than 9 percent. With his increased building program, Dönitz hoped to have 500 or 600 submarines in operation in a year or so. Then the British would be in for it!

In January came an event that once again changed the U-boat war against Britain. It had been triggered by events of the autumn of 1942. The Americans and British had increased the number and size of the Arctic convoys to Soviet Russia, and the Germans had responded by throwing more power against them. In September came Convoy PQ 18, a very large one protected by British aircraft carriers and many escorts. Admiral Raeder had detailed the big warships *Scheer*, *Köln*, and *Hipper* to attack the convoy, and Dönitz had four U-boats assigned to the task. The Luftwaffe had hundreds of Junkers 88s bombers and torpedo planes which were operating out of Norwegian bases. The German forces attacked. They sank four ships altogether. But they lost the *U-88,* the *U-457,* and more than twenty German bombers. The big capital ships did nothing at all in the fight. The same sort of performance occurred against other convoys; the big ships were just not quick enough. In December, Hitler observed that his vaunted surface navy was of virtually no use to him. Admiral Raeder got into an argument with Hitler about the employment of the big pocket battleships and cruisers. The Führer said these ships had proved themselves worthless in the battle of the Arctic, against the convoys to Soviet Russia. They were to be scrapped and the crews transferred to other activity. Raeder disagreed violently. What the Führer was proposing was the abandonment of the surface navy, he said. Exactly, said the Führer. Except for E-boats and destroyers, the surface navy was not worth a hoot.

Then the Führer would have to get someone else to run his navy, said Admiral Raeder. And he resigned as commander in chief. Hitler tried then, belatedly, to patch things up, but Raeder was not having it. Admiral Dönitz was chosen to be the leader of the German navy.

The choice meant that the Führer had begun to believe in the U-boat at last. Dönitz now had the opportunity to have his own way as January came. He continued to serve as commander of U-boats as well as commander of the entire navy. It was just a question of enlarging his staff.

The new year 1943 opened with 164 U-boats in the Atlantic, 24 in the Mediterranean, 121 in the Arctic, and 3 in the Black Sea.

One of Dönitz's first actions was to ask Hitler to release the boats in the Arctic for use in the Atlantic, where they could be so much more effective. He was persuasive, and Hitler let him have all but six of the Arctic U-boats.

Improved British communications and new routings of convoys puzzled the Germans in January, and the results were not good for the Germans. The British had improved their defenses enormously in the past year. Radar was one improvement: the escorts could track the submarines without the Asdic. RDF, radio direction finding, was another improvement in connection with the Americans. Huffduff was another. The Leigh light was still another—a powerful searchlight adapted for aircraft that both sought out the U-boat on the surface and blinded its gun crew as the Allied patrol bomber came in to attack. And in the offing was something else: the escort carrier. The British had been the first to use escort carriers in convoys, but the Americans, with their enormous productive capacity, were now turning out escort carriers in as little as a week's time. The British would have a dozen escort carriers this spring, and the Americans promised to provide another thirty before the end of June.

Now what did the escort carriers mean? They meant that the "Atlantic air gap" that had worked in the favor of the U-boats for so long would now be closed tight. There would be no area of the North Atlantic that would not be covered by aircraft, no place where the U-boats could feel safe from the prowling bombers. Dönitz had more U-boats out this winter than ever before, and yet the dangers to them were greater than before as well. Air cover, and as many as twenty escorts around a convoy, meant that the wolf packs were going to have new troubles.

But not quite yet. The day of the escort was yet to arrive. And as for new weapons, Dönitz had a few being developed as well. One was the Walter U-boat, something entirely new in design, which was in the development stage. It was powered by an engine that burned hydrogen peroxide, an easily obtained substance. And the principal difference between the Walter and the ordinary U-boat with electrical and diesel engines was that the Walter boat was a true submarine: it was built to spend its entire sea life under water. By the use of another development, the snorkel, the Walter boat could stay down from the moment it left port until the moment it returned. So if the convoys were to have all those escorts, the escorts would have to do some searching to find a boat that never surfaced. In this winter of 1943 all this change was on the horizon.

And as for aircraft, two could play at that game. The British were getting more and more long-range aircraft, and some American crews were also assigned to antisubmarine patrol on both sides of the Atlantic. Iceland was thoroughly covered. But so, too, out of Norway and southern France, were German patrol bomber squadrons flying to cooperate with the U-boats, to help them track down convoys, and to help them destroy the convoys once they were found.

In the Atlantic, it seemed to be a different story. On January 7, one of Dönitz's U-boats found a British convoy of tankers off the Canary Islands, bringing fuel to the Mediterranean. In four days, one of the admiral's wolf packs sank seven of the nine tankers, without losing a single U-boat. That was the sort of progress the admiral wanted to see.

But it was uneven progress. In attacks on one convoy the Germans lost three U-boats and four more were so damaged as to have to quit operating and go home. In February *U-69* and *U-201* found a convoy east of Newfoundland. Both submarines were sunk by the convoy escorts.

It became apparent to Dönitz that the enemy was finding his U-boats at sea long before they attacked, and somehow managing to evade many of them. Since the German *B-Dienst* had broken the British naval code, he was able to secure British U-Boat Situation Reports, put out by the Admiralty, and to see how very accurate the British readings were. He and his staff searched for the reason, and finally concluded that the new British radar was ever so effective. It could not be their codes, Dönitz said.

"We repeatedly checked our security instructions in order to ensure as far as possible that our intentions were not being betrayed. An efficient enemy intelligence service must have been able to ascertain the distribution of U-boats among the various bases, the dates of their sailing and return to port, and possibly also the sea areas allotted to boats proceeding on operations. Our ciphers were checked and rechecked, to make sure that they were unbreakable; and on each occasion the head of the Naval Intelligence Service at Naval High Command adhered to his opinion that it would be impossible for the enemy to decipher them."

The Germans did not learn until many years after the war that the accuracy of the radar was augmented by the breach of those most secret German codes by British intelligence. The Allies had had to be painstakingly cautious in their use of the material, ever careful to disguise the source, but at the bottom of Dönitz's troubles was this intelligence, the greatest single advantage the Allies were to have in this war against Hitler.

That advantage could not protect all the ships at sea, however, and the U-boat network was growing more powerful all the time. In February 1943, a wolf pack sank thirteen ships in Convoy SC 121 without losing a single U-boat. In March came a massive battle between two huge converging Allied convoys and three U-boat wolf packs, comprising thirty-eight U-boats. It came in the middle of that "air gap" in mid-

Atlantic that would soon disappear, but had not quite yet. The U-boats sank twenty-one ships and came as close to disrupting communications in the North Atlantic as they had ever done. But . . . without air cover, without any superweapons, the escorts sank one U-boat and damaged all the other thirty-seven, most of them so severely that they would be useless without major repair. That was the end of the long string of successes of Admiral Dönitz's U-boats. For a U-boat tracking a westbound convoy on March 26 observed something new: an aircraft carrier inside the escort screen of the convoy. When the U-boats of the pack came up, they found that any time they came within shooting distance of the convoy, there was an aircraft to force them down. The superior Allied radar did have its uses; when combined with the escort carriers it sounded the death knell of the U-boats.

10-1 Captain Achilles's *U-161* goes out from Lorient on what promises to be another successful patrol. It is always a time of excitement.
10-2 But this time (September 27, 1943), it is disaster for *U-161*. Off Bahia an American flying boat spots the U-boat and drops her depth charges, which force the diving submarine back to the surface. Eventually she sinks. The captain and all hands perish.

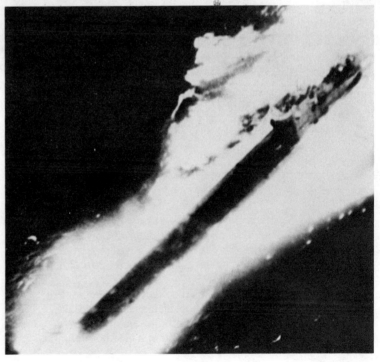

10-3 Admiral von Friedeburg inspects the
6th Flotilla at Wilhelmshaven. Von
Friedeburg is one of the unsung geniuses of
the U-boat war. At the last he managed the
U-boat campaign for Admiral Dönitz. **10-4**
The crew of *U-81* gets a welcome from an
Italian girl on coming into La Spezia from
patrol. **10-5** But not everyone could be in the
sunny South. The officers of *U-98* wonder
what to do about all that ice in the Baltic.
10-6 Captain Ulrich Folkers of *U-125*
watches the sinking of a steamer from the
bridge.

10-4

10-5

10-6

10-7

10-7 *U-125* was one of the Type IX boats that hit the American coast so hard in 1942 and again in 1943. Lieutenant Commander Folkers was unlucky: he ran into destroyers off Newfoundland, and they sank his ship. **10-8** A very pleasant evening, for Lieutenant Commander Ulrich Heyse at a reception in Bremen. Heyse took the first Metox radar detector to sea in September 1942, and after that the U-boats had a little better time of it against the improved British-American radar. He was later chief of the 32nd U-Boat Flotilla at Königsberg. **10-9** Admiral Raeder waves his grand admiral's baton at one of his U-boats as it puts to sea. **10-10** A distinguished group of U-boat officers. All of them distinguished themselves in action. At left is Hans Rösing, who won the Knight's Cross, and was later commander of U-boats in all the western area. At right is Fritz Frauenheim who, with Kretschmer, Endrass, and Schepke, waged so many successful wolf pack campaigns. He was later chief of the 29th U-Boat Flotilla.

10-8

10-9

10-10

10-11 By 1943 life had become so difficult for the U-boats that when they were not actually in the bomb-proof pens (rear) they had to be camouflaged even in the French ports. These nets are to make the boat look like a fishing smack from the air. **10-12** The *U-510,* a Type IX boat, enters Lorient harbor in the summer of 1943. Dönitz has already begun his program of rearming the U-boats. Note extra machine guns on bridge.

10-11

10-12

11. The Black Sea

German troops had moved down to the north coast of the Black Sea by the beginning of 1942, and it was not long afterward that Hitler decided U-boats should be sent into the Black Sea to sink Soviet ships. They were prohibited by Turkey's neutrality in the war from sending them around through the Mediterranean and through the Dardanelles and Bosporus. So the U-boats were shipped on a 2,400-kilometer land-sea voyage, up the Elbe to Dresden, over the autobahn to Regensburg, and along the Danube River to the Black Sea. By October 1942, the 30th U-Boat Flotilla was assembled at Constanza. It consisted of six of the little 250-ton "canoes": *U-9*, *U-18*, *U-19*, *U-20*, *U-23*, and *U-24*, and a force of 500 men. They had one hotel, one school, and one barracks. The chief of the flotilla was Lieutenant Rosenbaum.

In February 1943, *U-9*, *U-19*, *U-23*, and *U-24* were sent out along the Caucasus coast from Tuapse to Gelenchik to harry Soviet shipping. On February 14 Lieutenant Gaude's *U-19* sank the Soviet troop transport *Krasniy Profintern* and another transport. *U-24* sank the tanker *Soviet-skaya Neft*. *U-9* sank the tanker *Kreml*.

Sometimes the U-boats worked together along the coast with E-boats that had also been brought down from Germany. In March *U-24* sank a minesweeper. Lieutenant Fleige's *U-18* sank the steamer *Leningrad* and another unknown ship, and then the tanker *Vorosilov*. *U-19*, *U-20*, and *U-23* had no luck and returned to port emptyhanded.

On July 30 Lieutenant Peterson in *U-24* spotted the big Soviet tanker *Emba* in harbor at Suchumi. He torpedoed it, and it went to the bottom.

The U-boats also laid mines in Soviet harbors. In October 1943, the U-boats torpedoed a number of freighters near Poti and elsewhere along the Caucasus coast. They were masters of all they surveyed; the Soviets had no important defenses. One day, *U-18* came into the harbor at Batumi, and torpedoed a freighter as it lay at the pier. Not until April 1944 were there real indications of Soviet anti-U-boat activity. *U-23* encountered a Soviet minesweeper that month, which opened fire on the U-boat. On the surface they dueled, and *U-23* sank the minesweeper.

May 1944 was the high point of German U-boat success in the Black Sea. The five operating U-boats sank eleven Soviet vessels. June and July were not as productive, but *U-18* sank several vessels, including a tanker. Most of the ships these days were small coastal vessels, like the *Pestel,* which was rated at only 1,850 tons.

The end of the U-boats in the Black Sea came suddenly that summer, with the changing fortunes of the German army in the Caucasus. Soviet bombers visited Constanza and sank the *U-9.* The *U-18* and *U-24* were damaged so badly in this attack that they were not seaworthy.

Then the Red Army came driving toward Constanza on land, while the Soviet Danube Flotilla came from the sea. On August 24, the Germans evacuated Constanza. *U-18* and *U-24* were scuttled. Soon there were only two boats left in the Black Sea, the *U-23* and the *U-19.* The *U-23* as its last gasp torpedoed the steamer *Oituz* in Constanza, and then she was finished. The only U-boat left was the *U-19* under Lieutenant Ollenburg. On September 9, Ollenburg torpedoed the Soviet minesweeper *T410.* After that, there was no place to go. Constanza was in Soviet hands and, German ships having no friends on the Black Sea, Lieutenant Ollenburg headed for the Turkish coast. Outside Erkeli he scuttled the ship and the crew went ashore to be interned by the Turks. The brief Black Sea adventure was over.

11·1 Shipping the 250-ton "canoe" U-boats to the Black Sea. In 1942 they went by barge through the German internal waterway system, and then overland to Constanza. **11·2** Lieutenant Stodt, the skipper of *U-9*, one of the little boats employed against the Soviets in the Black Sea.

11-3

11-4

11-3 Constanza did not offer a great deal of recreation to the U-boat men. Mostly they had to make their own amusements. The result was frequent dinner parties with plenty of beer from home. **11-4** The *U-9* moves out of Constanza harbor on patrol against Soviet ships in the Caucasus.

11-5 *U-9* returns from patrol. The atmosphere down here in this forgotten corner of the world was much more relaxed than in the Mediterranean or the North Atlantic. The amount of enemy transport was not great, but there was virtually no opposition to the U-boats at first (see text). **11-6** Mail call at Constanza.

11·7

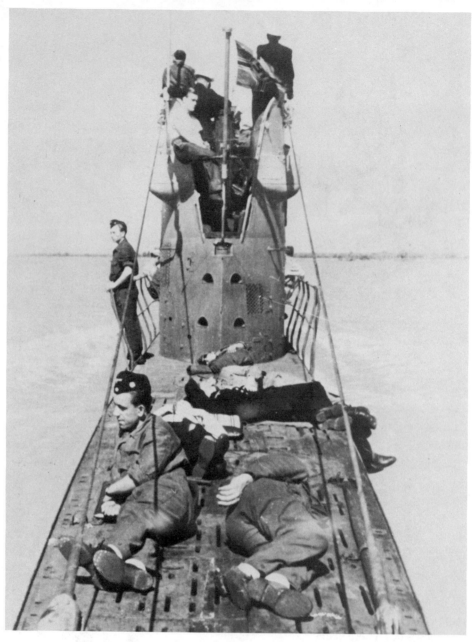

11·7 Patrol was largely a question of taking a sun bath. **11·8** *U-24*. The boat of the angry cat. Watch Officer Udo Hermann is at left, Lieutenant Commander Rosenbaum at right. Rosenbaum was commander of the 30th U-Boat Flotilla at Constanza.
11·9 Admiral Heye (back to camera) congratulates Skipper Klaus Peterson of the *U-24* after a successful patrol. At left is Lieutenant Commander Rosenbaum, with the Iron Cross at his throat.

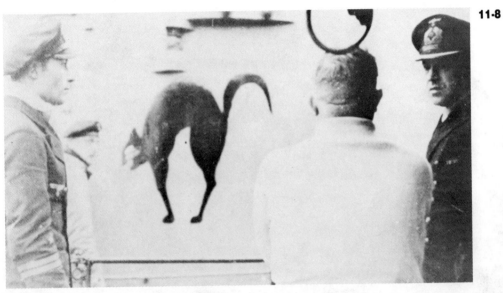

11-8

11-9

11-10

11-11

11-10 Skipper Peterson of the *U-24* and Skipper Hans-Ludwig Gaude of the *U-19,* at Constanza after the *U-24*'s sixth patrol, with flowers and unidentified girl. By the time the German U-boats were driven from the Black Sea in the spring of 1944, both skippers were long gone to other duty. **11-11** The little "canoe" *U-18* on patrol in the Black Sea.

12. The Tide Turns

April 1943 was the month in which the tide of the U-boat war turned. After that time, the U-boat threat was on the downgrade, and the U-boats were for a time as much hunted as hunters. And then they were more hunted.

The USS *Bogue,* a "jeep" carrier, was the first sighted by the U-boat skippers inside a convoy. She was anything but the last. By the spring of 1943 the convoys had all the air protections they could have requested: escort carriers, half a dozen hunter-killer escort groups provided by the British, long-range B-24 and PBY bombers to augment the Wellingtons and shorter-range bombers of Britain's Coastal Command, patrol bombers operating out of Iceland, surface and underwater radar, improved sonar and Asdic, the deadly Hedgehog, and, above all, these weapons in plenty.

At the end of March 1943 one of Dönitz's wolf packs found a convoy without much protection between the Canary Islands and the African coast. Attacks were made and three merchant ships were sunk. But that had been the result of an oversight by the Admiralty and it was quickly corrected. Air cover was rushed out to the convoy, and although the wolf pack chased the convoy for four more days, not one of the U-boats could come within striking distance, so effective was the air coverage. Nearly every U-boat involved was damaged by depth charges, and three were so badly damaged that they had to be withdrawn and sent back to Germany for repairs.

Looking around his world, Admiral Dönitz found weak spots in the Caribbean and off Cape Town. The *U-150* caught a convoy bound from Guiana to Trinidad and sank three ships in two days. There was another oversight. In African waters, *U-160* caught a convoy off Cape Town and sank four ships in a few days and damaged two more.

Lieutenant Commander Henke's *U-515* sank eight ships with a total tonnage of nearly 50,000. Certainly these were successes by the U-boats, but they were individual successes. In the North Atlantic, so many U-boats had been so badly damaged in the big convoy battles of early March that Dönitz did not have the boats to attack the convoys in early April. In mid-April the Wolf Pack Meise appeared off the Newfoundland coast. They did not do much. Convoy HX 233, which had been routed south by the Azores, was discovered by the Germans and they sent a pack of five boats against it. But in the battle that followed only one freighter was sunk by the U-boats and *U-176* was lost and several other boats were damaged.

From this point on, Dönitz noted that the British had much stronger escort services and the radar was so bothersome that on clear days the U-boats avoided the convoys. Lieutenant von Trotha in the *U-306* found Convoy HX 234 late in April in a heavy storm, and made the best use of the weather to attack. Four other boats joined. But even in storm, even with a wolf pack, only two ships were sunk, and the *U-189* and the *U-191* were both lost.

By May 1, Dönitz had recovered from the losses of those March convoy battles, and was able to put more than twenty boats in four wolf packs into the mid-Atlantic. On May 3 a convoy was discovered and then another, and the U-boats rushed in to attack. Immediately they seized an advantage and sank five ships. But five more destroyers were rushed out from Newfoundland and the No. 1 Escort Group also hurried up to help. By May 5, fifteen U-boats were in contact with the convoy, and from Berlin, where Dönitz now maintained his situation room, it looked like a night of good pickings. Twelve ships were sunk, but so were seven U-boats. Dönitz and his staff were shocked. The U-boat force could not bear this sort of loss.

Hoping that it was a fluke, Dönitz watched the operations of the next few days with extreme care. Convoy ON 184 set out with USS *Bogue* and five destroyers to cover. The weather was terrible and the *Bogue* could not launch planes for two days. The U-boats found the convoy and the wolf pack prepared to attack. But the third day dawned bright and clear, the *Bogue* put her planes up, and they found five U-boats. Four of them were attacked and driven under with various degrees of damage. *U-569* was forced to the surface and had to surrender, although Captain Johanssen managed to scuttle the boat and she sank. The HMCS *St. Laurent* picked up twenty-five survivors of a crew of fifty.

The U-boats hit Convoy SC 130 and Convoy HX 239 in force. They found themselves facing large and determined escort groups with very powerful radar, and constant air cover. The Hedgehogs and more powerful depth charges also shook the U-boat men. Their losses in the convoy battles were very high. At the end of the month, when Dönitz counted up his results, he saw that he had lost thirty-nine U-boats in May. Examining the evidence, Dönitz saw that he did not have the weapons to win in the Battle of the Atlantic, and he withdrew his boats. The new strategy was to hit and run wherever he might, until he could perfect his new types of U-boats that could remain constantly underwater, thus safe from discovery by aircraft and surface escorts. The battle of the convoys in the North Atlantic was over. Dönitz and his U-boats had lost.

With the increasing armament of the Allies and their ever-greater effectiveness against the U-boats, the tide changed steadily. In the spring of 1943 Dönitz was trying to combat the increased Allied air power, in particular, and more armament was being added to the boats.

The Type VII *U-450* was built at Danzig and went to sea for the first time in May 1943, under Lieutenant Boehme, a very young officer of the new school, who came from the ranks of the Hitler Youth and the new navy. The *U-450* was one of the last boats built without the second bridge gun platform. Her first war patrol was to Norway and she was in company with a tanker U-boat and the *U-449*. Off Norway they separated, and the *U-450* headed toward the Faroes to cross in the strait known to the Germans as "the rose garden" because it was the safest route into the North Atlantic. Their destination was the water off Iceland.

But safe, how safe? Here is what Radioman Kälsch of the *U-450* had to say about the voyage:

"We were not supposed to proceed on the surface at all. We had strict orders; 'Do not surface on any account.' That meant only to recharge our batteries.

"The first boat got through, that was the 'sea cow.' We heard from her, she received operational orders there. She got through splendidly.

I don't think we heard anything from the other one. Or did she go through after us? Then we went through, we got through perfectly. Once or twice we encountered aircraft, submerged away from it, but that's nothing to worry about. We got through and proceeded to a southwesterly course, which we were glad to do. It was Sunday, June 6. We had breakfast and we had two pastry cooks aboard. We had a fine spread at breakfast and we were supposed to be getting a first-class lunch. Suddenly at 10:50—one remembers the time afterward—aircraft were reported, and we, poor fools, with our single 2-centimeter gun up there. . . .

"I was sitting in the hydrophone room, encoding. Then they reported 'aircraft.' My radio mate was sitting in the radio shack. We looked at each other. The seamen rushed up on deck. There were only enough seamen up there to work the one gun. First of all we heard our gun firing, and then came a few bombs. The captain maneuvered splendidly. Hard to starboard, hard to port, maximum speed ahead on both engines. The bombs fell, first way off, then close, but they did practically nothing to the boat. He had apparently dropped all six bombs at the same time and had no more. Most of them were very wide. Inside things were only shaken up.

"Inside the U-boat it was quiet for a moment, but then we heard our gun rattling away again."

The aircraft had come back. It fired machine guns and cannon at the U-boat.

"After this second approach they were bringing down the wounded. I heard them dragging someone into the captain's cabin. There was an absolute pool of blood forward. Blood everywhere. This man was bleeding and at first I could not see who it was. I thought, Damnation that can't be the captain. It was the very devil when they got the captain. They laid him down and I saw it was not the captain but an ensign. We had two of them aboard that trip. [This was part of the hurry-up training program to create new U-boat officers.]

"This ensign and another had been manning the two machine guns on the deck, and one had been hit by a machine gun bullet when the aircraft flew not more than thirty feet over the conning tower. They could see the British laughing at them up there.

"The captain was standing on the bridge in his white cap. The aircraft flew over and fired again. The boatswain's mate manning the 2-centimeter gun suddenly crumpled. The second man took over, the aircraft came back, and he too was wounded. The third man took over, and he managed to hit the aircraft with a burst. The plane turned off diagonally, and the captain ordered the U-boat to dive.''

They made a clean getaway, if one could call it that. Half a dozen men had been wounded, including the captain, who was hit in the right hand. The first watch officer was also wounded in the leg.

They stayed down at 90 feet all the rest of the day. Then they headed back to port. Six men went into the hospital. The first watch officer had suffered a severed tendon; when he came out one leg was shorter than the other and he was finished in U-boats.

The second lieutenant then became first lieutenant. But the next time they sailed, they again encountered aircraft, this time 1,600 miles from their new base at Brest.

It was midday. The battle with the aircraft lasted twenty minutes. The captain was wounded. The new first lieutenant was shot in the eye, and was blinded for several days. He was also shot in the arm. This time so many men were wounded in the air attack that "it was like a hospital ship: an ensign (the most seriously wounded) was in the captain's cabin. Number one was in the petty officers' quarters. Number two, number three, and the Captain were in the bow compartment. We had no ship's surgeon, and no medical corpsman. There was only one seaman who was a chemist by civil profession, and he looked after everyone.

"The engineer officer was now in charge of the boat. He had a helluva time. Half an hour had elapsed since our escape. We were at 75 feet. Then we were hit by two bombs. Most of us were in the bow compartment. We had just started to eat. We were still very shaken and numbed by what had happened. The bombs wouldn't have mattered a damn but having the wounded there did. What were we to do now? Should we proceed to base, or hand them over to another boat, or what were we to do?"

The engineer officer was considering that problem when the men heard a sudden explosion. Radioman Kälsch thought first that the men aft were smashing up things. The plate fell from his hands. After another explosion, all dropped their plates and rushed aft. The boat was going down by the bows. Then she started up again, and then down. It had been another aircraft bombing, and it had knocked out the fuses. Once they were put to rights, the boat could be put on an even keel. But the damage was such that they went back to base. Another patrol without result.

The tales they heard at Brest were enough to curl their hair. One boat went out on deep diving exercises and never came back. Two direct hits from torpedoes, fired by a British submarine!

The captain left the *U-450* then, to go into the hospital, and Lieutenant Gerlach took over. He was not yet twenty-two, the youngest captain in the German U-boat navy. But one patrol, and he was transferred to another boat.

"Crazy," said Radioman Kälsch. "No one knew what was going on."

In March, the *U-450* went out again, Skipper Boehme commanding. Once more they encountered aircraft, and one attack so damaged their ballast tanks that when they wanted to maintain depth underwater they had to use the main pump to keep water in the tanks. On March 10 they encountered a convoy and moved in to attack. But up came a British destroyer and the *U-450* submerged to 120 feet. The destroyer moved off—or so it seemed. Then, through the hydrophones, the Germans heard three ships approaching. This was the new method of attack by the escort groups, possible in 1944 because the British and Americans had built so many escorts.

The *U-450* went deeper. The pump was turned on.

"One is approaching again," said the hydrophone operator. "She's coming slowly."

"Keep pumping" said the skipper. The men kept pumping and the noise, a hiss and roar in the control room, seemed almost deafening, much worse than the sound of flooding.

Every man was tense, what with all that noise and the enemy approaching again.

Then a lead from the number-three ballast tank gave way, and water began coming into the control room. It could not be stopped.

The enemy ships came closer and began dropping depth charges. They fell very close, and the boat fell off and went out of control. More water began coming in through the number-three ballast tank. Soon the water was knee-deep in the control room, and the fathometer registered 600 feet. The pump was working furiously.

"Watch the depth," yelled the engineer officer. Tanks were blown and the boat went up to 300 feet. She had just reached the 300-foot level when another depth charge attack came down, and one charge must have exploded right on the bow.

"Now she'll break up," thought Radioman Kälsch.

"Don life jackets," shouted the captain. He ordered the boat to the surface. But when the *U-450* hit the surface she headed right back down again, out of control. Back down to 300 feet before finally the captain got her under control. All that maneuvering had apparently thrown the British off the track. But the boat was damaged beyond repair. She was no longer watertight, and only by running the pump could she be kept down.

The skipper took her a little way farther and then ordered the boat to surface.

"The destroyers have gone," he said. "All hands prepare to abandon ship."

The crew then went up on deck. There were plenty of rubber dinghies so they could get off in style. About half the crew was on the deck when two destroyers came back in sight, one on the starboard side, the other on the port. There was no escape.

The destroyers began by firing signals. Then they fired their guns. They were firing too short.

"All hands forward of the conning tower," yelled the captain.

The destroyers kept coming. Men began dropping off the boat into the water. "Come on, we're clearing off," they shouted, and they threw in the dinghies.

So in a very disorderly fashion, with no order given by the captain, the crew of the *U-450* abandoned ship. The engineer was the last man off, having stopped to set the scuttling charges. He also opened the caps of the four bow torpedo tubes, the air vents and the flooding flaps. As the last men left, the British got the range, and the shells began smacking into the submarine. A shell hit the bridge, and set it afire. The scuttling charges went off, but still the boat settled ever so slowly, because she had no way on her.

"What a sight it was," said Radioman Kälsch. "The sun had just risen. It was five o'clock in the morning. The sun looked so beautiful and the sky was slightly reddish in the dawn. The bridge was burning. What a spectacle! The two destroyers fired from afar, and then the third one came in. They came straight toward our boat. They didn't bother about the crew for a moment, they thought they could still capture the boat. The first destroyer immediately put out a boat with hawsers and everything.

" 'Damnation,' we kept saying, 'won't the boat ever sink?' "

"Then the bows went down. Then it suddenly went faster. The conning tower was submerged. The stern rose up, and that was the end. She sank before the British could make fast to her."

The men of *U-450* became prisoners of war.

In June 1943 Dönitz faced a bleak future. If he carried on the U-boat war, he knew the losses would be more than the gains. He called in his senior commanders: Captain Rösing, commander of submarines west, Commander Lehmann-Willenbrock of the 9th Flotilla, Commander Kuhnke of the 120th Flotilla, Commander Sohler of the 7th Flotilla, Commander Schultze of the 6th Flotilla, and Commander Zapp of the 3rd Flotilla. They conferred and agreed that the U-boat war must go on, even with expectable losses of enormous proportions, until the day when the entirely submersible U-boat would be ready. At the moment all they could do was strengthen their defenses, especially air, and improve their techniques for survival.

In the past two years the U-boat force had suffered from the expansion that brought so many new men into U-boats. There was no time now, with the need to meet ever-growing losses, to go back to the leisurely training methods of the past. So the *Agru Front* had been developed as a training device. It was a sort of obstacle course for new U-boat crews. When a boat had been launched and fitted out, and gone to sea for trials, the *Agru Front* scheme went into effect. At least one officer and several petty officers and enlisted men in each new crew were agents of *Agru Front*. Their duty was to try to create dangerous situations within the boat that would force the crews to respond with all they had learned. For example, the order might be given to crash-dive, and the diving officer, an *Agru Front* man, might set the diving planes at so acute an angle that the boat would crash to the bottom if it were not stopped. The captain and the rest of the crew had to discover the sabotage and correct it. Or a petty officer might leave a valve open, or a torpedo-tube cap might be loosened. Every sort of disaster that might overtake the submarine was considered and as many tricks as possible were played on the crew until they were well aware of the problems of survival. It was not the best sort of program, and it meant that many half-trained crews were going to sea, but with the demands on Dönitz's training programs, it was the best that could be devised.

Dönitz now set about perfecting his defenses. The U-boat pens had been built in 1940 and 1941. Lorient, La Pallice, Saint-Nazaire, Brest, Bordeaux, the German bases at Heligoland, Wilhelmshaven, and Kiel, and those at Narvik and Trondheim and other Norwegian points were all *impregnable*. The British, who in the summer of 1943 were bombing the German U-boat bases, had waited too long. But once a boat left the pens it was in danger. One step taken in 1943 was to rebuild the bridges of the U-boats, adding strength and high-powered antiaircraft guns. Another step was to build "flak traps," which looked like ordinary U-boats, but whose upper decks were actually gun platforms bristling with guns. They had two 2-centimeter four-barreled guns, and one semi-automatic 3.7-centimeter quick-firing cannon.

On May 23, 1943, the *U-441*, the first of these "aircraft traps," sailed from Brest. On May 24 a Sunderland flying boat attacked the *U-441*, and was shot down, but not before the Sunderland had dropped its bombs, which damaged the *U-441* so much that she had to return to base.

So far a standoff.

On June 8, however, the *U-758* was out, similarly armed. She was attacked by a Lysander bomber, and drove it off with heavy damage. The Lysander dropped smoke flares near the U-boat before it left. Then up came another Lysander and a Martlet fighter, which stood well off and attacked but did not score any damage. Still another Martlet came up later, delivered a low-level attack and bombed, and then was hit and fell into the sea. Then along came two Mustangs, which attacked. One was hurt and returned to its base. But another replaced it in the attack. Finally the skipper of *U-758* had enough damage so that he decided to call the fight off and submerged. He said it was a victory, and perhaps it was. But as the Germans had now discovered, the British and Americans had an awesome lot of aircraft.

And the sad fact was that no matter what defensive tactics the Germans tried, the Allies were closing in on them in the Bay of Biscay. More escorts, operating in groups, guarded the exits from the harbors. The Germans took to convoying submarines out in groups, with surface craft. That helped. But enemy escorts and aircraft ganged up on them still. One group of five outward-bound boats found itself beset by four fighter bombers. *U-545* and *U-63* were so badly damaged that they had to return to base.

In June 1943, the British reinforced their blockade with a number of new antisubmarine hunter-killer groups. German losses in the bay began to rise. At the end of July when two U-boat groups sailed, Dönitz ordered destroyers to accompany them to sea. All seemed to go well. But the next day one of the U-boats reported she was in battle with five enemy aircraft 125 miles north of Cape Ortegal, on the northern coast of Spain. So many aircraft were reported around the bay that Dönitz stopped all further sailings until he could assess the situation. And when it was assessed he learned that between July 20 and August 1 ten boats had been lost on the way out to sea, without firing a torpedo.

The tactics had to be changed. No longer would the boats try to fight their way out on the surface. They would dive and stay under all the time, surfacing only at night to charge batteries, and then with the greatest care.

The Germans had also been working on their own radar system, and, although they were far behind the Allies, had developed one that helped identify incoming aircraft and attacking escorts.

So the battle went on, but now the odds were with the Allies.

Dönitz was also waiting for other developments to mature. One was the Walter U-boat, developed by Helmuth Walter. He had been working on the design and engineering since 1934. The first prototype had been built at the Germaniawerft factory in Kiel in 1940. That boat could make 26 knots under water compared to the 9 knots of the ordinary U-boat. But OKW, the supreme military command of German armed forces, decreed that this was too risky. They were doing just fine with the Type VII Atlantic boats just then (1940), and OKW refused permission to move toward production on the Walter boat and insisted that the Type VIIs be the mainstay of the German forces.

By the fall of 1942 renewed arguments for the Walter boat still had not resulted in its adoption, but a certain flexibility had come about. So a compromise was made, and production began for two new types of boat, Type XXIII, a small boat suitable for work in the North Sea and British estuaries, and Type XXI, a very large boat, suitable for trans-atlantic crossings. It had one major improvement over the old U-boats, a snorkel, or breathing device, which permitted the boat to remain underwater for days, even weeks, taking in fresh air and expelling gases through the breathing device. These boats would be ready for action at the end of 1944. Just now, Dönitz had to get along with what he had, with such modifications as he could devise to be added in a few days.

His answer was to send U-boats to places where the Allies did not concentrate their power. The war at sea had been a game of cat and mouse, with the U-boat as the cat. But now it was a game of dog and hawk and cat, and the U-boat cat was very much at a disadvantage. The U-boat was still a dangerous weapon, but as long as the Allies had plenty of sea and air power, the danger from the U-boats was cut way down. There was no longer any question of Dönitz winning the Battle of the Atlantic. All he could do now was hold on, and wait for his new supersubmarines to be ready.

12-1 After the beginning of 1943 the trip in and out of such western French ports as Lorient became extremely dangerous. On August 7 planes from the American escort carrier *Card* found the *U-66* and the *U-117* together. They sank the *U-117*. The *U-66* survived for another year before being sunk off the Cape Verde Islands. **12-2** The *U-81* at Salamis in the fall of 1943. This was the boat that had sunk the *Ark Royal* two years earlier. A few weeks later she was sunk at the Italian naval base at Pola by an aircraft.

12-1

12-2

12-3

12-4

12-3 The *U-97* puts out to sea on June 5, 1943. One day later she was attacked by aircraft near Haifa in the Mediterranean, and . . .
12-4 . . . there is the wreckage of the *U-97* stranded on the beach.

12-5

12-6

12-5 The plight of the U-boats kept getting more serious. The day is August 11, 1943, off Ascension Island. The second U-boat (background), the *U-604*, has been scuttled by her crew following severe damage by an air attack. The crew (in water and aboard *U-604)* is being rescued by the men of *U-172.* **12-6** When the men of the *U-604* reached the *U-172* they needed help getting up.

12-8

12-7 The long patrol. The *U-177* went out into the South Atlantic, heading for the Indian Ocean, on April 1, 1943, and did not return to port until October 1. She was fed by milk cows and German surface raiders. Captain Robert Gysae is at right, hatless. **12-8** Skipper Gysae already had his *Ritterkreuz;* while on this patrol he was awarded the oak leaves. **12-9** Medals or not, much of his time was spent at the periscope.

12-7

12-9

12·10 A beautiful day in the South Atlantic at high speed. The U-boat men called this *Marschfahrt.* **12·11** Manning the gun against incoming aircraft. **12·12** The *U-177* sinks the SS *Alice F. Palmer,* July 10, 1943.

12·11

12·12

12-13 A Martin PBM navy patrol bomber takes off. These planes were instrumental in finding and destroying U-boats. **12-14** TBF Avengers in formation. These navy torpedo bombers were also used as carrier antisubmarine patrol planes, and carried depth charges.

12-13

12-14

12-15 A PBY, long-range patrol bomber of the sort used to find U-boats offshore, on patrol. **12-16** An escort carrier. The introduction of these ships into convoys in the middle of World War II brought the swift end of the U-boat threat to the Atlantic lifeline. **12-17** A light carrier at sea, its deck loaded with aircraft. These carriers also increased the threat to the U-boats.

12-16

12-17

12-18

12-18 The *U-185* goes down, torpedoed by an antisubmarine patrol plane from the USS *Core,* one of the escort carriers that changed the odds in the war of the Atlantic. **12-19** But the Germans continued to launch U-boats. Here the *U-209* goes down the ways.

12-19

12·20

12·20 The *U-217* was a lucky ship. This hole in her bow was made by a depth charge that did not penetrate the inner hull no matter how severe the damage looks from outside. **12·21** Sinking the steamer *Rhexenor.*

12·21

12-22

12-23

12-24

12-26 The *U-460,* one of Dönitz's milk cow submarines, Type XIV, which seemed to have so much promise. Nine of them were launched, but by the middle of 1944 all had been sunk. The *U-460* was just too slow to escape an attack by planes from the U.S. escort carrier *Card,* and she sank on October 4, 1943.

12-22 When two survivors showed up in a leaky lifeboat, there was nothing to do but rescue them. **12-23** One of the rescued men was a ship's officer, Mr. Allen. Here he is on the bridge with Captain Reichenbach-Klinke. **12-24** In borrowed clothing, Mr. Allen leaves the *U-217* at Brest, at the end of the patrol. Next time Skipper Reichenbach-Klinke took her out, they were not so lucky. The *U-217* was sunk in the Atlantic by an American airplane from the USS *Bogue,* another escort carrier. There were no survivors. **12-25** Sometimes a U-boat was lucky in an encounter with an American torpedo plane. The *U-264* made it back to Saint-Nazaire in October 1943 from her fourth war patrol after her bow was shot off. But on her next patrol, she was sunk on February 19 by a British hunter-killer team.

12-26

12-29

12-27 A delicate maneuver. Moving torpedoes from the *U-462*, a milk cow, to one of the operational submarines at sea. **12-28** The *U-62* undergoing *Agru Front* training at Kiel. Several members of the crew were detailed to "sabotage" the U-boat and it was the job of the new captain and his U-boat men to stop them. **12-29** Burial at sea aboard the *U-462*. Skipper Vowe comes down from the bridge to read the service. Air attack was the usual reason for injury and death of one or two men. Most of the crew of the *U-462* avoided this watery fate. Lieutenant Vowe's boat and the *U-461* were both sunk on July 30, 1943, just a few miles from each other off Spain's Cape Ortegal, by aircraft from two different RAF squadrons. Most of the crews were rescued and made prisoners of war.

12-30

12-30 And still they kept coming. . . . Officers and men of the *U-566* stand for inspection at Lorient. Note the bombed-out buildings in back. In 1943 and 1944 the Allies made enormous efforts to destroy the U-boat pens, but all they did was destroy the towns around them, and make life difficult for everyone, but not impossible for the U-boat force. **12-31** Some of the beards were superb.

12-31

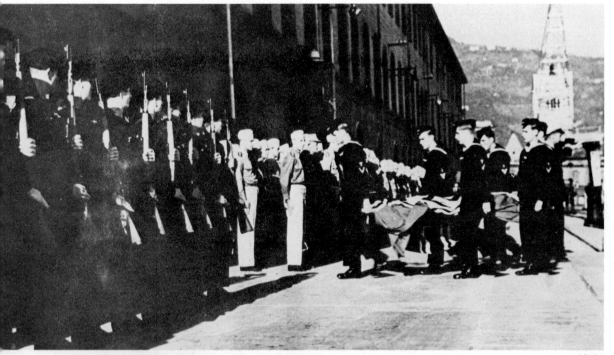

12-32

12-33

12-32 An honor guard for the funeral of U-boat man Horst Saupe at La Spezia, Italy. **12-33** On May 6, 1944, the USS *Bulkeley* rammed and sank the *U-66* at sea. This is what ramming a U-boat does to a destroyer's bow.

13. U-Boats Abroad

After Admiral Dönitz realized he had been defeated in the Battle of the Atlantic, he decided to send his U-boats out to the far-flung waters of the British Empire, to strike his enemies where they were not likely to have such sophisticated defenses. The Japanese had been suggesting joint submarine operations with the Germans in the Indian Ocean and Pacific. They were particularly interested in such German developments as the snorkel. They had offered Dönitz bases at Penang and Sabang in Malaya for operations in the Indian Ocean. In the spring of 1943 the Japanese began building a base at Penang.

Dönitz had dragged his feet as long as the Battle of the Atlantic seemed to be proceeding well, but after the March 1943 battles, he agreed to the Japanese proposal. So he decided to send a number of IX-C and IX-D2 U-boats to the Far East. The IX-C was a big boat, 76 meters long, with twin diesel engines and twin electric motors. She carried twenty-two torpedoes or sixty-six mines, and a deck gun of 10.5 centimeters. She also had one to four 2-centimeter antiaircraft guns and one 3.7-centimeter flak gun. Her crew numbered forty-eight men.

The IX-D2 was one-fourth larger and 10 meters longer, and could carry twenty-four torpedoes. She had four 2-centimeter guns, one 3.7-centimeter gun, and a crew of fifty-seven men.

Dönitz decided to send out some thirty boats. The idea was to get them into the Indian Ocean before the summer monsoon, so they sailed in June. As hoped, they surprised the British, and on their passages, outward and home, they sank fifty-seven ships. But, when the count was finally made, Dönitz also lost twenty-two of these big U-boats, most of them to aircraft and most of them in the Atlantic on the way out or on the way home.

Dönitz also sent U-boats out to work off the African and South American coasts. This entailed the use of the Type XIV tankers, the milk cows, and turned out to be a dangerous and ultimately unsatisfying business, for, as noted, the tanker's one great disadvantage was its slowness in responding to signals for a crash dive, and so in the end all of the tankers were sunk.

The first group of U-boats to go out east was Group Monsoon I, which set sail that summer from the western French ports. Eleven boats set out, but only five of them reached the Indian Ocean. *U-532* sank four ships and damaged another. *U-188, U-168,* and *U-183* also sank ships, as did *U-533*. But *U-533* was sunk by an aircraft in the Persian Gulf on October 16. The others all managed to reach Penang and establish the base there. They also based at Surabaya.

The second Group Monsoon set out at the end of 1943. Sixteen U-boats began the voyage and they had better luck about getting there. The most adventurous voyage was that of Commander Kentrat, whose *U-196* made the longest cruise of any U-boat in the entire war, 150 days.

Two German surface tankers were sent out to service the U-boats in the east, but both were sunk: the *Charlotte Schliemann,* scuttled when attacked by the destroyer *Relentless* on February 12, 1944; and the *Brake* by a hunter-killer team.

Two of those U-boats that reached Penang were sent home loaded with tin and rubber: *U-178* and *U-188.* By the end of 1943 the base was established, under Commander Wilhelm Dommes. The U-boats moved around quite a bit, traveling to Japan and to Java, where the *U-859* and *U-861* operated out of Djakarta. The *U-168,* one of the earliest boats to go out east, was unlucky enough to encounter the Dutch submarine *Zwaadvish* one day in June 1944, and was sent to the bottom. The *U-181* worked out of Djakarta and on November 2 sank the American tanker *Fort Lee.* Captain Schrewe's *U-537,* also operating out of Surabaya, was sunk by the American submarine *Flounder* that same month. The *U-196,* which had been transferred over from Captain Kentrat to Captain Spiegler, went out one November day and was never heard from again.

After the long voyage out, and operations in the east, the *U-843* started home, reached the Kattegat off the Swedish coast, and was sunk there by an Allied aircraft, virtually in sight of the homeland.

The U-boats traveled far. *U-862* went around the coast of Australia and off Sydney sank an American Liberty ship, traveled clear around, and sank another Liberty ship off Perth.

The return of the last German U-boats in East Asian waters began on January 6, 1945. The first boat was the *U-510* under Captain Eick. On February 23 she sank the steamer *Point Pleasant Park,* and headed toward Germany. But on April 24, off Saint-Nazaire, she ran out of fuel and had to surrender. Next boat was the *U-532.* She sank two ships on the way home and was still at sea when the capitulation of Germany was announced. She steamed into Liverpool and gave herself up.

U-843 and *U-861* made it back to Bergen. *U-183* under Captain Schneewind was sunk in April 1945 by the American submarine *Besugo.*

The last boat to go out to East Asia was the *U-234,* which sailed from Kiel under Captain Fehler on March 23, 1945. She was a Type X-B boat, a minelayer. She carried a load of mines, and several extra passengers, including the German air attaché to Tokyo. She was hit by a torpedo and sunk off the Norwegian coast, but brought up, repaired, and sent out again. She set out, this time traveling under water by snorkel, toward the Faroes and the Iceland passage. After the capitulation, she changed course, and ended up surrendering in Portsmouth, New Hampshire.

Of the rest of the Asia fleet of U-boats, the *U-181, U-195, U-219,* and *U-862* remained in Japan and were taken over by the Japanese. They were renamed *I-501, I-502, I-506,* and *I-505.* After V-J Day the first two surrendered in Singapore, the other two in Djakarta.

13-1 In the summer of 1943 a number of U-boats were sent by Dönitz to East Asia to cooperate with the Japanese (see text). Here the crew of one of the U-boats is inspected by a Japanese general.

13-2 Kapitän-Leutnant Ibbeken of the *U-178* with Commander Klaus Scholtz, commander of the 12th U-Boat Flotilla, on the dock alongside the boat at Bordeaux in 1943. A few days later the *U-178* set out for Penang. She made the trip safely.

13-3 In Penang the men of the *U-178* met their Japanese counterparts. Loaded with tin and rubber, the *U-178* returned to Bordeaux in 1944 and Skipper Ibbeken went ashore. Lieutenant Commander Spahr took over that summer, and was in charge on August 20 when the American drive through France threatened Bordeaux. He scuttled the boat.

13-1

13-2

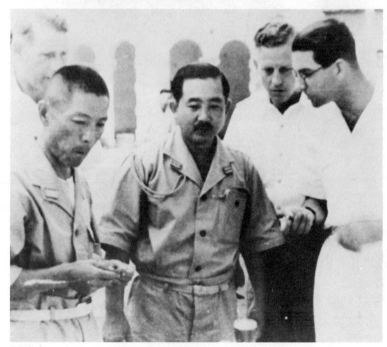

13-3

13-4 These are the most modern rockets of 1943, aboard the *U-511,* a Type IX-C boat which Skipper Schneewind took to Japan that year. **13-5** Comrades. Three U-boat men with a Japanese submariner. The Japanese were not used to seeing U-boats in their part of the world, and by error the Japanese *RO-500* sank the *U-511* in September 1943. **13-6** Skipper Schneewind survived, returned to Germany, and brought the *U-183* to Japan. It was a long voyage, from November 1944 to February 1945. The boat was fitted out with more room for amenities than those operating in home waters.

13-5

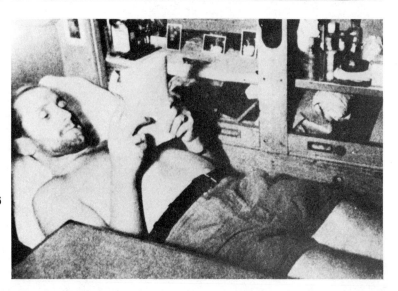

13-6

13-7

13-8

13-7 The *U-183* arrives at Osaka in February 1945. 13-8 There were many ceremonial dinners. The man standing, left, is the official Japanese-German interpreter. Seated in front of him is Skipper Schneewind, looking grave as the admiral makes his speech. The *U-183* then went down into the Java Sea to operate against the Americans, but was caught on the surface by the U.S. submarine *Besugo* on April 23, 1945, and sunk.

13-9

13-9 When the *U-180* visited Japan, Subhas Chandra Bose, the misguided Indian nationalist leader, was there. Bose had broken away from the Congress Party of Gandhi and Nehru in the mistaken belief that the Japanese would serve India's interests better. This is one of the few pictures ever taken of him, aboard the *U-180*. He died in a plane crash on Formosa in 1945. **13-10** Here are the skippers of all the U-boats that were going out in the first wave from the French ports for the far reaches of Asia. At the moment it seemed a welcome adventure.

13-10

14. The Last Days

The worse things got for Germany in 1944 and 1945, the less trouble Admiral Dönitz had with Hitler. Dönitz was counting on his new "supersubmarines" to stem the tide, and Hitler had always favored "superweapons" like the buzz-bombs and the V-1 and V-2 rockets that were unleashed against England. Thus, said the Führer, he would bring England to her knees. He was saying this even in the spring of 1945, and, remarkably, many in Germany were still believing him, including those brave but naïve men of the U-boat corps. So in 1944 and until the bitter end, the U-boat corps was vigorously trying new weapons.

One such, which Dönitz put into action during the Normandy invasion of June 6, 1944, was the "one-man torpedo." Unlike the Japanese *kaiten*—the submarine hull with a torpedo for a warhead instead of a bow, which operated in the Pacific—the German one-man boat was a real submarine with a torpedo suspended beneath it. The operator could fire the torpedo when he wished, and then escape from the area. But enemy domination of the air around France made it impossible to move the boats and move supplies into position, and so the one-man torpedoes were of virtually no use.

Seventeen U-boats were stationed at Brest when the invasion began. Fourteen were in Saint-Nazaire, four in La Pallice, and one in Lorient. They tried to get into the action but *U-971, U-1191, U-269,* and *U-988* were sunk, and six other boats were so badly damaged that they had to retreat to their bases.

The air-sea antisubmarine campaign of those early hours of the invasion is one of the untold stories of World War II.

In all, Admiral Dönitz reported that between June 6 and August 31, thirty U-boats equipped with snorkels had taken part in forty-five operations. They sank five escorts, 12 merchant ships, and four landing craft. Twenty of the U-boats were lost, which also meant a thousand men. That was an almost vessel-for-vessel exchange, and yet so far had even Dönitz retreated from reality by this time that he tried to put a good face on it in terms of what the supplies lost to the Allies would have meant to the German war effort!

As of the invasion, Dönitz ordered that no more U-boats were to go out without snorkels. The *Graf von Matuschka* took the *U-482* out into the North Channel, north of Ireland. There he lay on the bottom waiting for ships to come by, playing dead, with only the snorkel coming up to breathe for the boat. The tactic was quite successful, and he sank a corvette and four merchantmen on this patrol. But on the next patrol, in the same waters, a British hunter-killer group found the *U-482,* and sank her. Lieutenant Roth's *U-1232* had better luck. She sank a number of British ships off Halifax, and ultimately her crew survived the war.

By this time the snorkel was in general production and virtually all boats were adapted with it. *U-124* and *U-218* set out with mines and snorkels to lay a minefield around Plymouth harbor. But the successes of the U-boats were few. *U-480* sank two barges and two ships, but was herself sunk by a British corvette in the English Channel.

Early in August, the Americans broke out of the Cotentin Peninsula and that meant the end of the U-boat bases in western France. Some boats managed to get out and escape to Norway, but many were caught and scuttled by their crews before the Allies could reach and capture the bases. By September, which marked the beginning of the fifth year of the war for the Germans, they had lost 248 U-boats. Between this time and the end of the war, that figure would nearly be quadrupled, as the Allies overwhelmed Western Europe.

If the U-boats were of no use in trying to stem the invasion of Europe, at least they continued to be effective to an extent in their operations against the English ports. Still, the whole emphasis of the war had changed. In the old days the boats might remain at sea for sixty days, and of these forty were operational. Now the boats might go out for an average of thirty-seven days, of which only nine were operational. The difference was that, since they were traveling underwater with the snorkel, as they had to do to avoid detection, they were much slower. And the results showed in the very small amount of shipping that was sunk after June

1944. Dönitz was still fighting his holding action, waiting for the super-weapons.

One by one the superweapons showed up. The snorkel caused the Allies a great deal of difficulty. In November 1944, the loss of shipping, which had declined to well below the 100,000-ton mark, suddenly shot up above 100,000. Sir Andrew Cunningham, the First Sea Lord of Britain's Royal Navy, expressed serious concern to the War Cabinet and asked that more effort be made to destroy U-boat bases and U-boat construction facilities.

And then, in the winter of 1944–45, came worse news for the British. The two new U-boat types, XXI and XXIII, were reportedly ready for action and would soon be appearing from the German shipyards in large numbers. The Type XXI was the oceangoing boat, bigger than anything else the Germans had built. It had a rubber skin, which deflected radar and Asdic. It had a large battery which could run the boat for four days with one charging. It never need surface, courtesy of the snorkel. It had a new radar which was much improved. It used the acoustic torpedo as standard. This torpedo need only be fired in the general direction of a vessel, and it homed in on the propeller noises and virtually never missed. Later it would be bettered by still another torpedo, the Lut, that could be fired in any direction and would then home in on the vessel in great concentric circles. A Type XXI boat could fire six of these Lut torpedoes in one moment, from 160 feet beneath the surface.

The British had responded to the acoustic torpedo by streaming paravanes behind their ships to attract the acoustic features. But the paravanes (little propellers that made real propeller noises) destroyed the British Asdic results, which made it harder to find the submarine.

By the beginning of January 1945, the British were really scared. Admiral Cunningham (who had dropped into a perpetual state of panic) predicted that Dönitz would be able to mount a new submarine offensive with sixty Type XXI boats and no one knew how many Type XXIII boats, and that the number of Type XXI boats would increase to ninety by spring. Was it to be the U-boat war all over again?

But Admiral Cunningham need not really have worried so much (and Prime Minister Churchill was his beaming and most unworried self), for the land war was progressing so rapidly that the best estimates of Dönitz's engineers were as nought. Instead of thirty Type XXI boats in January, the Germans had two, which would be ready for trials in February. They did have a dozen or so Type XXIII boats in the shallow waters around Britain—boats that were very much like the little 250-ton canoes of the past, except that they had the snorkel and the Lut torpedo. They would lie in wait in the shallows for incoming convoys, and raise hob with them; but still in the winter months of 1945 the submarines never sank more than 65,000 tons of shipping in any month. Did not the British remember those days when 700,000 tons in a month had been the figure?

No, Dönitz was not going to win the war for Germany at this late date. It was true that the Type XXI and the Type XXIII submarines were the finest in the world, and why not? The German naval experts had concentrated on submarines all during the war while the Allies were devoting their efforts to many other devices that in the end won the war for them.

When it all ended in May 1945, and the German U-boats surrendered en masse or scuttled themselves, 140 Type XXI boats had been launched, but very few of them were actually in service, and there were 61 Type XXIII boats. Only one of the superboats was actually ready to go. She was the *U-2511,* and in May 1945 Lieutenant Commander Adelbert Schnee had her out in the Atlantic ready to fight. He had come up through the Skagerrak and the Kattegat and the Norwegian bases, and he had headed up north in the time-honored way and had reached the Faroe Islands. On the day that Admiral Dönitz was negotiating the capitulation, Captain Schnee was looking for game, and just had found it, a British cruiser in his periscope, when came the order from Dönitz: cease all military activity.

14-1 The snorkel, housed. Extended it could breathe from below normal periscope depth, giving the U-boat a new life underwater. The boat never had to surface from the time it set out on its war patrol until it returned. **14-2** A Type XXIII boat on a training cruise (see text)

14-3

14-3 Even after the tide had turned against Germany, there were benefits to being in the U-boat force. Here one of the crew cleans fish for the dinner of the crew of *U-490.* **14-4** The *U-234,* showing her snorkel partly extended. **14-5** On July 8, 1944, Captain Maertens's *U-243* was caught by aircraft west of Nantes, France, and sunk. **14-6** The survivors of the *U-243* were picked up by HMCS *Restigouche.* Note men in water behind destroyer.

14-4

14-5

14-6

14-7

14-7 Captain Schumann-Hindenberg of *U-245* with improved direction finding equipment. It must have worked, for the *U-245* survived to be destroyed by the British at the end of the war. 14-8 How great the snorkel. A U-boat cartoonist depicts a Type XXIII boat just outside London. The top legend is "War Patrol." The bottom says "That's how it is on the snorkel patrol."

14-8

14-9

14-9 But here's how it really was by the beginning of 1945. A British minesweeper has just attacked the *U-300* off the Spanish coast (February 21, 1945) and forced her to the surface. **14-10** The crew of the *U-300* is rescued by the British from their sinking U-boat.

14-10

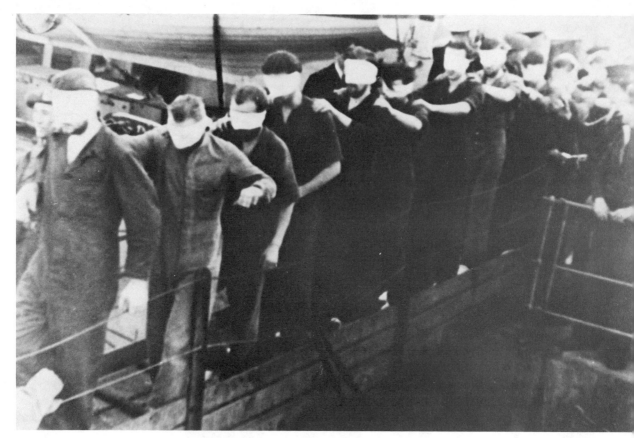

14-11

14-11 Coming ashore. The *U-300* men were blindfolded when they came ashore at Gibraltar after capture. The treatment of captives was largely a matter for the discretion of the captain of the capturing vessel. It was a tribute to the U-boat force that the skipper of this ship felt they were still very dangerous, even after their boat was sunk.

14-12

14-12 Oberleutnant zur See Selle and the small crew of the *U-795*. This boat was a Type XVII U-boat (see appendix), just coming into service at the end of the war, a Walter *Versuchboot* (search boat). Only five were launched and none of them ever got into action, a fact for which the Allies could be thankful. They had all the new weapons developed by 1945, plus a virtually noiseless hydrogen peroxide engine. Note how young the crew was, and how small a crew was needed. The Allies didn't really ever get a good look at the finished product because all the Type XVII and Type XVIII Walter boats were scuttled at the time of the capitulation.

14-13 Even at the end: the building of still another U-boat. **14-14** A Type XXI boat sunk in Hamburg harbor after the "bombing storm." On March 30, 1945, the U.S. Eighth Air Force staged major bombing raids on Wilhelmshaven, Hamburg, and Bremen. They destroyed fourteen U-boats. The British returned on April 8 to destroy more. **14-15** A Type XXI U-boat making her trials. **14-16** Three Type XXI U-boats at Kiel. **14-17** Type XXI U-boats ready for sea.

14-13

14-14

14-15

14-16

14-17

14-18

14-19

14-18 The crew of one of the Type XXI boats prepares for inspection by Grand Admiral Dönitz in the spring of 1945. **14-19** Captain Adelbert Schnee (see text). At the end of the war, Captain Schnee was out in his Type XXI boat, the only one really ready for action, on his way to the American coast, when he got the word that the war was over. **14-20** Captain Peter Cremer accepts official congratulations on his return from a successful cruise. He was one of the lucky ones who survived the war. His *U-333* ran up one of the most impressive records of the U-boat corps. **14-21** One that survived the war. The *U-57,* which bore this red devil insignia, survived the entire war, to be sunk by Lieutenant Kühl and his crew on May 3, 1945, at Kiel. **14-22** After the surrender at Weymouth, England, Captain Uwekock (white hat) of the *U-249* and two of his officers (rear) look glum enough. The British tars in foreground are too busy to care.

14-20

14-21

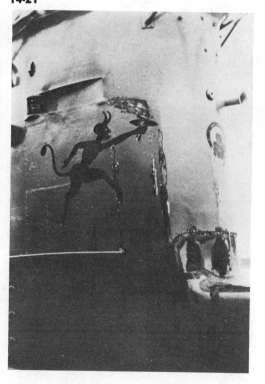

14-22

14-23

DIE ENTSTEHUNG DES ROTEN TEUFELS AUF U-93 UND U-57

Der Kommandant, Kapitänleutnant Claus KORTH, schreibt:

"Ein Turmwappen mußten wir haben, das war ja ganz klar. Die Schwie= rigkeit blieb, wer soll= te es entwerfen ? In der ganzen Besatzung hatte ich nur einen,der zur Fachschaft - Bil = dender Künste - hätte gehören können, den Masch.Gefr. SATTLER.Der mußte es schaffen. S. malte auf meinen Befehl zwei Tage lang Wappen= entwürfe. Seine Schla= ger blieben dabei be= zaubernde Mädchenköpfe und Teufel, wie man sie sich wilder nicht hätte vorstellen können. Ich wollte zu gerne einen Haifisch mit aufgesperr= tem Rachen haben, der zwischen seinen Zähnen etwas ein Schiff zermalmt, vielleicht auch

Mr. CHURCHILL.

Doch mein Sattler hatte noch in seinem ganzen Leben keinen Haifisch gesehen, und meine künstlerische Idee fiel damit leider unter den Tisch. Da ja ein Mäd=

DER ROTE TEUFEL AUF
U93 UND U57

chenkopf wirklich nicht als Wappen auf einen U-Boot-Turm paßt, suchte ich mir den wildesten Teufel aus, denn von fremder Hand wollten wir uns das Wappen nicht malen lassen. Das ging gegen unseren Stolz. So wurde unser Wappen geboren. Der Künst= ler erhielt dafür den Namen "Iwan der Schreckliche". Wir aber steuern seitdem mit seinem fackelschwingenden - ROTEN TEUFEL - gegen England.

Später wurde ein neues Wappen von Oblt.z.S. v. HARTMANN, der ein geschickter Zeichner war, an den Turm gemalt. Denn so ganz ohne roten Teufel wollten wir doch nicht bleiben. Unser Wappen sieht etwas anders aus. Der jetzige rote Teufel fängt listig lächelnd mit einem Kätscher einen Dapfer, in dem Mr. Churchill, die unvermeidliche Zigarre rauchend, ahnungslos daher fährt."

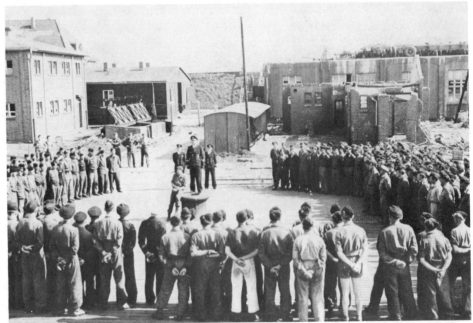

14-25

14-26

14-23 This broadside was distributed among the U-boat men in the early days of the war, when this little Type II-C "canoe" was the standard submarine operating in the North Sea. The gist of the text is that Winston Churchill is properly horrified at the power of the red devils and that perhaps they will take him into custody soon. **14-24** Surrendered U-boats lined up at Londonderry, May 1945. **14-25** The U-boat men at Wilhelmshaven listen to their commander after capitulation to the Allies, May 1945. Note bombed-out buildings around parade ground. **14-26** The U-boats near the American side at the announcement of surrender headed for the U.S. shore. Their welcome was not very warm. Men of the *U-1228, U-873, U-234,* and *U-805* were promptly clapped into cells in the marine detention barracks at Portsmouth, N.H. **14-27** The *U-234* just after she was blown up by the United States Navy in 1946.

14-27

14-28

14-28 Dönitz in a formal pose as commander in chief, with his baton. **14-29** Survivors and families of the old U-boat men come to pay homage at the memorial at Möltenort, near Kiel—all civilians now. **14-30** Admiral Dönitz, as commander in chief of the German navy, 1945.

14-29

14-30

Epilogue

Out of the disaster that Hitler's Third Reich became in the last weeks of the war, the U-boat force stood out because of its unflagging efforts to bring victory to a failing Germany. All this effort, all this hope lay behind one man, Grand Admiral Karl Dönitz, who to the very last moment held the respect of everyone in Germany and most of all his U-bootwaffe. Dönitz, as a Prussian officer, was thought to have transcended Nazism and the quarreling of the Nazi vultures over the political corpse of Hitler in the last days. When it came down to the last, and Hitler had to turn the reins of government over to someone, he bypassed all the party faithful (unfaithful most of them), and entrusted the fortunes of a failing Germany to the one man he trusted as a leader: Admiral Dönitz.

Dönitz knew as well as anyone how desperate was Germany's situation. He also knew that there was no hope for the U-boat war, that the submarines could no longer turn the tide, no matter what his subordinates said. In the last weeks, Dönitz himself took resources from the U-boat war to bring strength to the east, and to try to save the population of eastern Germany by moving the people away from the face of the Soviet attack. When Hitler announced the "scorched earth" policy, Dönitz quietly subverted it in the port cities.

On April 30, Dönitz was finally appointed total head of state (Göring, who coveted the job, had tried a coup d'état and had been outlawed by Hitler). Dönitz then presided over the surrender and had to accept the dismemberment of Germany.

The war over, Admiral Dönitz was tried, along with Göring and the other major Nazi leaders, for war crimes. He claimed that he knew nothing of the Nazi atrocities against Jews, Russians, Poles, and others, a claim that might have been true, for Dönitz's whole life, almost to the end of the war, was bound up in the navy, and particularly in his U-boats. But, of course, he had to be convicted. He was sentenced to life in prison and remained a prisoner for most of the rest of his life, being released a few months before his death.

The U-boat force was, of course, disbanded and the U-boat men were split among the two Germanies. But in the increase of international tensions, U-boat forces grew up in both Germanies, and by the 1980s the Federal Republic of Germany had U-boats of its own once again, operating under the NATO navy a U-boat force that honors the memory of Admiral Karl Dönitz as a war strategist once again, and this time with the concurrence of his enemies of the past.

Appendix

Before and during World War II the Germans produced, or planned, many different varieties of U-boats.

Type	Description	Displacement*
Type I-A	high seas U-boat	1200 cbm
Type II-A	coast U-boat	381 cbm
Type II-B	coast U-boat	414 cbm
Type II-C	coast U-boat	435 cbm
Type II-D	coast U-boat	460 cbm
Type III	high seas U-boat; not built	
Type IV	planned, but not built	
Type V	planned, but not built	
Type VI	planned, but not built	
Type VII-A	high seas U-boat, Atlantic	915 cbm
Type VII-B		1040 cbm
Type VII-C		1070 cbm
Type VII-D		1285 cbm
Type VII-E	planned, but not built	
Type VII-F		1345 cbm
Type VIII	projected	
Type IX-A	transocean U-boat	1408 cbm
Type IX-B		1430 cbm
Type IX-C		1540 cbm
Type IX-D1		2150 cbm
Type IX-D2		2150 cbm

*1 cbm = 1 cubic meter.

Type X-A	high seas minelayer; not built	
Type X-B	high seas minelayer and supply ship	2710 cbm
Type XI	U-cruiser; not built	
Type XII	fleet U-boat; planned, not built	
Type XIII	small combat boat; projected	
Type XIV	fuel transport	2300 cbm
Type XV	large torpedo transport; not built	
Type XVI	large torpedo transport; not built	
Type XVII	Walter search boat	280 cbm
Type XVIII	Walter high seas boat†	1887 cbm
Type XIX	fuel freighter; not built	
Type XX	large oil transport‡	3245 cbm
Type XXI	electroboat, transocean	2114 cbm
Type XXII	small battle boat; not built	
Type XXIII	small electroboat	275 cbm
Type XXIV	large battle boat; projected only	
Type XXV	coast U-boat; projected only	
Type XXVI	Walter high seas turbine boat	1160 cbm
Type XXVII-A	small U-boat "Hecht"§	12.25 cbm
Type XXVII-B	small boat "Seehund"	14.9 cbm
Type XXVIII	coast U-boat, steam-turbine-driven	200 cbm

Other U-boats were still in the conceptual stage, but no building had been done.

†This boat was building at war's end.
‡This boat was building at war's end. It differs from the Type XIV in purpose. The Type XIV was built to supply the U-boats. The Type XX was to transport oil for the armed forces.
§ The Hecht and the Seehund were miniature U-boats for one- and two-man crews, but not suicide boats.

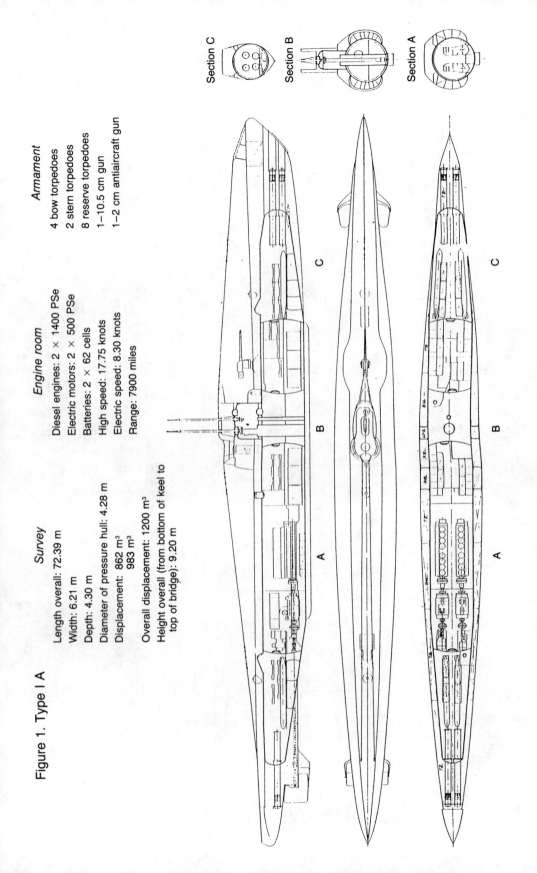

Figure 1. Type I A

Survey

Length overall: 72.39 m
Width: 6.21 m
Depth: 4.30 m
Diameter of pressure hull: 4.28 m
Displacement: 862 m³
983 m³

Overall displacement: 1200 m³
Height overall (from bottom of keel to top of bridge): 9.20 m

Engine room

Diesel engines: 2 × 1400 PSe
Electric motors: 2 × 500 PSe
Batteries: 2 × 62 cells
High speed: 17.75 knots
Electric speed: 8.30 knots
Range: 7900 miles

Armament

4 bow torpedoes
2 stern torpedoes
8 reserve torpedoes
1–10.5 cm gun
1–2 cm antiaircraft gun

Section C

Section B

Section A

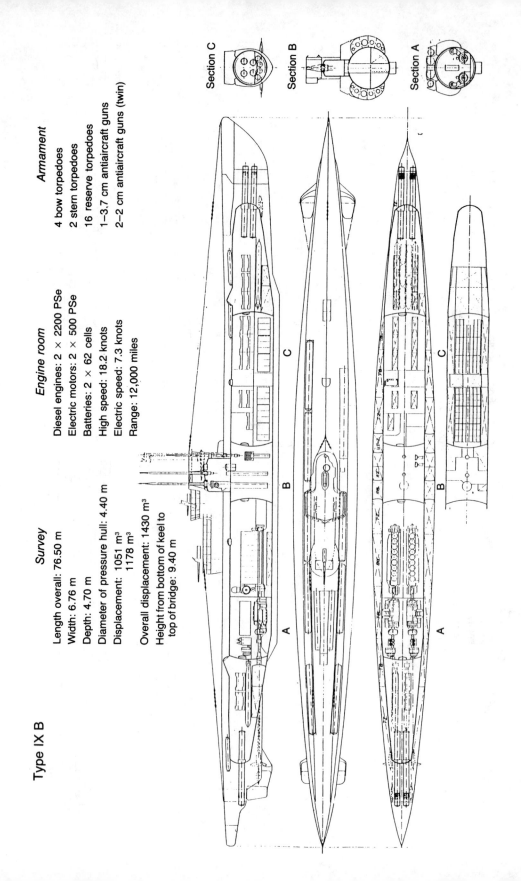

Type IX B

Survey

Length overall: 76.50 m
Width: 6.76 m
Depth: 4.70 m
Diameter of pressure hull: 4.40 m
Displacement: 1051 m³
1178 m³

Overall displacement: 1430 m³
Height from bottom of keel to
top of bridge: 9.40 m

Engine room

Diesel engines: 2 × 2200 PSe
Electric motors: 2 × 500 PSe
Batteries: 2 × 62 cells
High speed: 18.2 knots
Electric speed: 7.3 knots
Range: 12,000 miles

Armament

4 bow torpedoes
2 stern torpedoes
16 reserve torpedoes
1–3.7 cm antiaircraft guns
2–2 cm antiaircraft guns (twin)

Section C

Section B

Section A

Type XIV Submarine Tanker

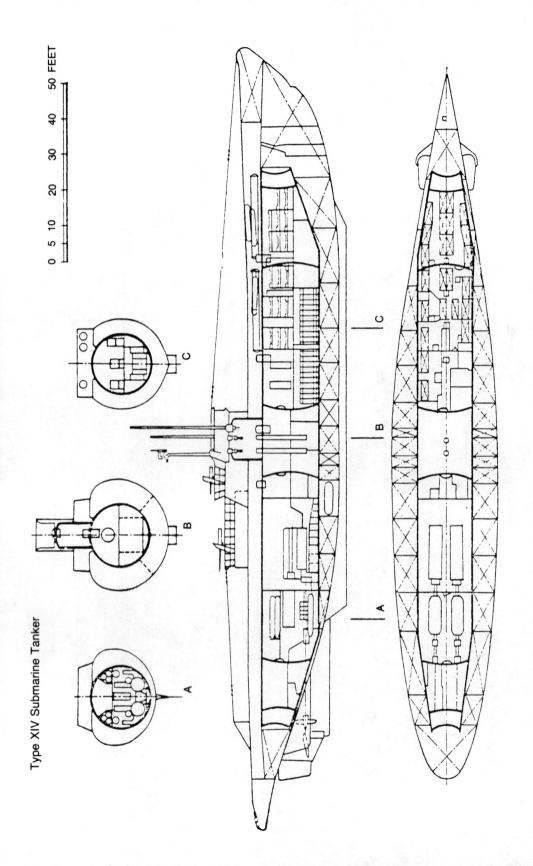

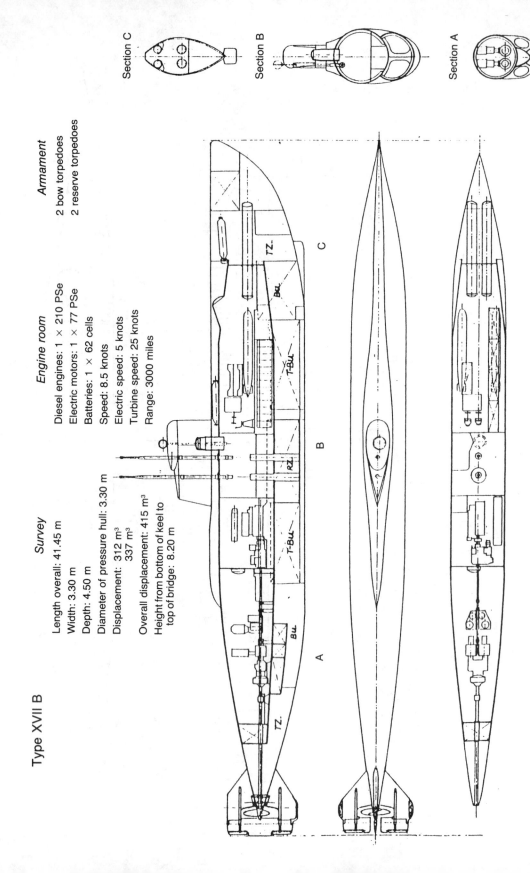

Type XVII B

Survey

Length overall: 41.45 m
Width: 3.30 m
Depth: 4.50 m
Diameter of pressure hull: 3.30 m
Displacement: 312 m³
              337 m³
Overall displacement: 415 m³
Height from bottom of keel to
top of bridge: 8.20 m

Engine room

Diesel engines: 1 × 210 PSe
Electric motors: 1 × 77 PSe
Batteries: 1 × 62 cells
Speed: 8.5 knots
Electric speed: 5 knots
Turbine speed: 25 knots
Range: 3000 miles

Armament

2 bow torpedoes
2 reserve torpedoes

Section C

Section B

Section A

Type XXIII

Armament

2 bow torpedoes

Survey

Length overall: 34.68 m

Width: 3.00 m

Depth: 3.66 m

Diameter of pressure hull: 3.00 m

Displacement: 232 m³
256 m³

Overall: 274 m³

Height from keel to top
of bridge: 7.40 m

Engine room

Diesel: 1 × 575 PSe

Electric: 1 × 580 PSe

Batteries: 1 × 62 cells

High speed: 9.7 knots
13.1 knots

Range: 2800 miles

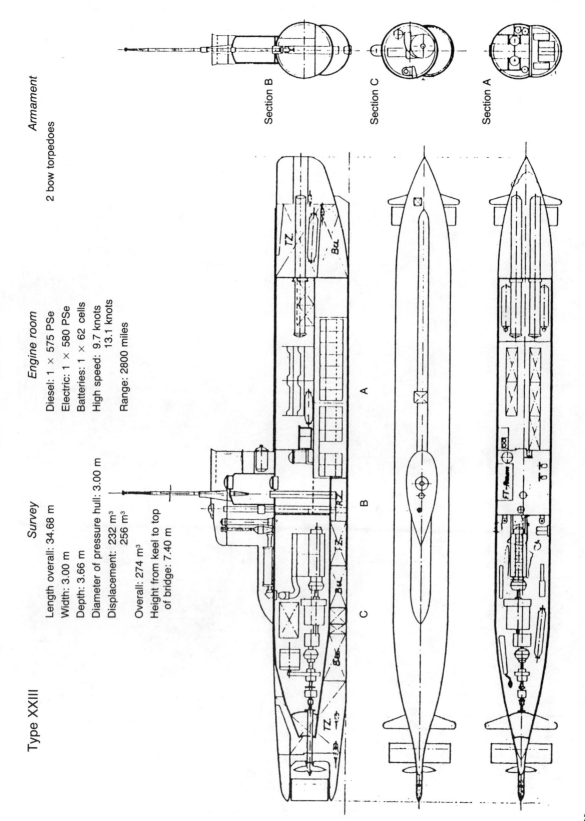

Section B

Section C

Section A

Index

ABOUT THE AUTHOR

Edwin Palmer Hoyt III is a writer, journalist, and historian who was a war correspondent in Asia and the Middle East. He has been, variously, news editor for the U.S. Office of War Information in China and a member of their psychological warfare team in India and Burma; reporter, editor, and writer for the *Denver Post* and *San Francisco Chronicle*; and a producer-director-writer for CBS News TV. His numerous books include *Japan's War, Guadalcanal, The Kamikazes, U-Boats Offshore,* and *The Militarists*. Mr. Hoyt lives in Maryland.